SOMEONE'S SURVIVAL GUIDE

Empower Yourself with Real-Life Wisdom: Discover Inspiring Breast Cancer Survivor Stories and Practical Advice

Philip Alderson
The Breast Cancer Community

Ballyhoo Designs

Copyright © 2024 Philip Alderson

All rights reserved. No part of this compilation may be utilised or reproduced by any means, graphic, electronic, or mechanical, including photocopying, recording, taping, or by any information storage and retrieval system, without the explicit written permission of the copyright owner(s), except in the case of brief quotations incorporated into critical articles and reviews. Due to the constantly evolving nature of digital content, any web addresses or links included in this compilation might have changed since its creation and could no longer be current or accessible. The opinions and viewpoints expressed in this compilation solely belong to their respective authors, and they do not necessarily represent the opinions or perspectives of the compiler or publisher. The publisher disclaims any liability for the expressed viewpoints.

Contact: Philip Alderson -- phil@ballyhoodesigns.co.uk

Someone's Survival Guide / Philip Alderson -- V 1.0

ISBN: 9798873624737

Cover design by: Philip Alderson

CONTENTS

Title Page
Copyright
INTRODUCTION
Following the Authors   1
Teresa   3
Rachel Hanley   5
Mandy Chard   9
Liz Venus   11
Georgi   13
Lisa Alford   15
Tabby Luxmoore-styles   19
Claire Minidriver   29
Jo Knight   31
Phil Alderson   33
Kari Bastian   37
Gina Davidson   39
Karla Cornwall   45
Lisa Fleming   47
Martina   49

Sam Cummins	51
Preeti	55
Jeannie	57
Chantel Chantiluke	59
Nicola Collings	61
Dr Liz O'Riordan	63
Claire Woolger	65
Karlina Louise	67
Gemma Bradbury	69
Charlotte Rose	73
nikki j	75
Stephanie Arnold	77
Cindy Beehler	79
Vanessa Thacker	83
Laura McGowan	87
Aimée	89
Patti Carey	91
Helen Smedley	93
Natalie Mizuik	95
Kelly	99
Susie	101
Kath Hamilton	103
Kathy Paulson	105
Jo Hayes	107
Laura Ashurst	109
Gemma Haydock	111

Nikki Scott	113
KATIE	115
Fiona	117
Jessica Aidem	119
Jo Hammond	121
Sam Parr	125
Carly Moosah	127
Mia Davies	129
Jodi Holland	131
Emma Young	133
Dawn Jehle	135
Gaye Noble-Wootton	139
Diane Castro	143
Bisbrooke Artisans	145
Aliki Dar	147
Kelsie Davies	151
Sinead Gravill	153
Diandra	155
Alex Perry	157
Joely A. Serino	161
Natalie Whipps	163
Sam Everett	165
Hayley Gullen	169
Hannah Louise	171
Clare Etherton	173
Rhiannon Vickerman	175

Laura Middleton-Hughes	177
Carrie-anne Callan	179
Cheryl Thompson	181
Melissa Golding	183
Doug E Harper	185
Afterword	187

INTRODUCTION

Welcome to this extraordinary compilation of resilience, hope, and triumph in the face of adversity. As a male breast cancer survivor, I am honoured to introduce this remarkable book, 'Someone's Survival Guide,' crafted from the heartrending, inspiring narratives of breast cancer survivors worldwide.

Within these pages, you'll discover a mosaic of experiences, shared by individuals—some newly diagnosed, others seasoned survivors—who have walked the path of uncertainty and emerged with invaluable insights. Their stories, tips, and strategies serve as a guiding light for those facing the daunting diagnosis of breast cancer.

Brene Brown once said, "One day your story will become someone else's survival guide." These profound words echo the heartbeat of this book and sparked the very idea behind its creation. Each contributor to this anthology has embraced this sentiment wholeheartedly, turning their personal narratives into beacons of guidance for others navigating the turbulent waters of a breast cancer diagnosis.

Assembling this anthology has been an arduous yet deeply fulfilling journey. The collaborative efforts of these courageous survivors have resulted in a compendium of not just words, but emotions, courage, and unwavering determination. Their contributions extend beyond prose; some have even curated soundtracks designed to uplift and motivate.

This book stands as a testament to the resilience of the human spirit and the unbreakable bonds forged within the breast cancer community. It is my sincere hope that the stories and wisdom shared here will serve as companions through the darkest moments, offering solace, guidance, and the assurance that one is never alone in this journey.

'Someone's Survival Guide' is a labor of love, a testament to the power of unity, and a beacon illuminating the way toward increased awareness and early diagnosis. It marks just the beginning—a catalyst for the change needed to halt cancer in its tracks.

May this book not only inspire but ignite a global movement toward eradicating breast cancer. Together, let us create a legacy of empowerment and support for survivors, leaving an indelible mark on the fight against this disease.

With unwavering hope and determination,

Philip Alderson - @philaldo - Male Breast Cancer Survivor

FOLLOWING THE AUTHORS

A Shortcut Into The Breast Cancer Community

Discover more about our courageous contributors by exploring their stories and journeys on Instagram. Each author's Instagram handle, listed under their name, serves as a direct link to their personal accounts.

Follow these handles to delve deeper into their inspiring narratives, connect with their experiences, and find a supportive community of survivors sharing wisdom and hope beyond the pages of this book.

Join us in celebrating their strength and resilience by engaging with their empowering stories online.

*This book is not affiliated with or endorsed by Google Inc. Google and the Google logo are registered trademarks of Google LLC. Any references to Google services, products, or trademarks are used solely for informational purposes and do not imply any partnership or endorsement

PHILIP ALDERSON

TERESA

@mademoiselle_vert

No profound tips or words of wisdom from me. This wasn't my first tango with BC but even I learned a few things, some of which are below:

* Being scared is normal

* It's okay to ask for help

* It's okay to ask your Doctors questions and query things.

*Write down your concerns as they pop into your head, it makes it easier at appointments.

* Reach out to the BC community. It is a shit club to be part of but one full of amazing people.

* If having chemo it is wise to invest in a baby toothbrush, baby toothpaste, and bonjela

*Lastly, do it your way. We are all unique and individuals.

Teresa - @mademoiselle_vert

PHILIP ALDERSON

RACHEL HANLEY

@rachel_x_ann

C ancer …the gift that keeps giving and taking, but, there is light in the dark times ahead of what one must face and endure, and my hope for you reading this, is that you will find glimmers of sunshine and joy in those everyday moments once more, and keep making amazing and cherished memories.

In my early stage diagnosis of 2011, aged 40, I wish I could have foreseen the future, but then I would have missed out on my own personal growth and spiritual awakening as my cancer journey unfolded.

Through the blur of tears I understand that I needed to walk through the whole of my messy, complicated, yet beautiful story to become who I am today.

I want to establish some of the mixed emotions I once had; of grief following my mastectomy surgery, chemo hair loss, and a life that once was.

Consuming fear from living my life tinged with the worry of recurrence, or metastasis, was further impacted by seeing my bestie and other dear souls taken by Metastatic B-reast C-ancer.

The honest truth is, I was drifting... searching for 'something', looking for 'purpose'; it was like cancer had stolen my identity, and I was tired and weary from doing everything in my own strength with Dr Google by my side.

Limping along with some renewed enthusiasm I began to settle into my new normal when, in January 2017, I was confronted with my worst fear, and a new diagnosis that gave validation for me to crumble.

However, I knew I didn't want to go back to the dark place I had once been.

To rise strong above this next storm I needed to search deep within my heart and soul. It was as if something was shifting within my spirit, despite the now incurable diagnosis of stage 4, metastatic breast cancer, with a forever treatment plan for the future.

Lovingly, I have forgiven and released all of the past which has healed my hurting heart.

My diminished Faith with the God of the universe has been rekindled and In May of 2017, whilst on chemo and with no hair, I shared my testimony with church, family and friends, and was baptised.

It feels now rather like I have reset my life; both as a mum, and now overseas supporting my husband in his career here in Switzerland.

I have let go of the worry and fear that consumed me and I see the world through the lens of a hope in Jesus.

It does not exempt me from pain and anxiety, but rather

the new version of me has an inner peace and calm to better handle this ongoing cancer journey.

There isn't a handbook of how to 'do cancer', but in this amazing world I am thankful to be able to connect with a vibrant tribe of community who get it.

So reach out, love is all around you to gently guide you and walk by your side.

Whether that is from a support group, charitable organisation, or via social media platforms, there is an abundance of knowledge and quality advice 24/7.

Nobody ever needs to walk alone

Rachel Hanley - @rachel_x_ann

PHILIP ALDERSON

MANDY CHARD

@mrsachard

19/08/2017 - Exactly a year since my biopsy results and my surgeon told me I had cancer, since she said it had spread into my lymph nodes, that I would have to have an operation, chemotherapy and radiotherapy.

Its been a year of contradictions. In some respects it has dragged, but in others it feels like it has flown by. It's a year I will look back on and memories will be blurry due to the shock, the fear of the first few days and weeks, and then the drugs and the whirlwind of treatments and hospital appointments.

Treatment is hard going and you have to deal with it a day at a time, look too far ahead and the fear takes over.

I'm not the same person I was before cancer and although I'm trying really hard to get back to 'normal', my old 'normal' doesn't fit me anymore. I'm not sure what that means for my future yet and that in itself is quite scary.

What I've learned is that the struggle isn't over once treatment finishes. I may now be able to say I'm in remission but the battles in my head have just started and I also need to find some healing in my heart.

I ache for the old me, I don't think I'll ever get her back and I'm grieving, at the same time I feel strangely fortunate to have changed in the ways I have. To have stared down my own mortality and been marked by the experience in a way that makes me appreciate what's truly important and that life is so fleeting. It may seem strange to be grateful to cancer but I guess there is an element of that.

I only hope I find the right future which enables me to live the rest of my life however much of it I have left in the way I now want to.

Unfortunately society has a way of pulling you back to what is deemed acceptable and whilst I may be dreaming of seeing the world, taking stock and breathing on the top of a mountain, or sitting watching a stunning sunset on a beautiful beach that isn't realistic.

How sad are the ties that bind us to the material, it's not how things should be.

Mandy Chard - @mrsachard

LIZ VENUS

@liz_thickandthinmainlythin

Surviving Cancer With A Few Other Health Friends

My survival advice as a breast cancer patient who has other life limiting health conditions:

Having been told by my oncologist and the MDT team for three months I was not well enough to have any neo adjuvant treatments, in my mind there was only one option left and so I took medical retirement from my career in order to prioritise my health. It was my passion and I was proud of the job I did but it was demanding and left little time for me. Things had to change.

I then rested, ate really healthily, exercised gently and slept the clock round. It was during the pandemic and so I avoided anywhere and everyone.

I decided instead of having to be busy seeing, doing, going, I was just going to do 'being' instead.

Proof positive it worked because 3 months later I had the go - ahead for surgery, chemo and radiotherapy.

Instead of the death sentence I felt I'd been handed, it was the best news .

I sailed through it all, surprising all of my medical team and I'm still here to tell the tale.

Life is very different now, quieter slower paced but I'm still proud of myself but for different reasons. I ensure my health and wellbeing and that of my family comes first and I wouldn't change it one bit.

Liz Venus - @liz_thickandthinmainlythin

GEORGI

@booby_business

This Is A Story Of Hope After The Death Of Your Husband/Wife/Partner...

My husband Craig died on the 20th of January 2009 aged 39. He was diagnosed with a rare cancer 7 years before and given approx 2 years to live.

For 7 years, I lived knowing he was going to leave me. Everything we planned would be lost and gone, all of our hopes and dreams.

Anticipatory grief is weird. You know it's coming. You're just not sure when, and when it does, it surprises you.

There is no rulebook, there is no time limit, and your grief is not the same as others.

Don't be afraid to admit that there is a sense of relief in death. That the fear, worry, and anxiety of the time building up to death has stopped. That the unknown is now known, and that the reality may not be as you expected.

Death is final for the person that has died, but it is never final for the person left behind.

Remember, though, that life is still there for you, and you deserve to live. Don't be afraid to smile, laugh, and cry. Crying will come at the times you least expect it, yet the times you think you'll be a wreck, you'll be okay.

People will come and go, life will be hectic for a while, then it will be empty, really empty.

Emptiness is a void, a huge black hole, a space that is hard to fill, something that unless you've been there you can't explain.

Nights go on forever, 6 pm until 6 am, and there are 12 hours of nothing. How do you fill that time when the one you shared that time with for so long is no longer there?

Don't rush to fill the space, the void, the emptiness. Let it be, let it grow, and let it be normal, whatever normal is now.

Life will continue, friendships that you thought were your forever friends may fade, you'll no longer be part of the group as you're now single. The invites will stop coming, and you may feel sad, hurt, and upset.

Anger hits. You'll be angry that they died, angry that you're left, angry that your life will never be what you thought it would be. Let the anger be, let it take hold for a while, go with it, then let it go.

You'll make mistakes, I made some epic ones, but that's okay.

Georgi - @booby_business

LISA ALFORD

@ljalford71

Following my diagnosis on 22/08/22 and when acceptance had set in I decided to pull my big girl pants up and take control of what was to come.

I read, researched, joined forums, scoured websites and reached out to other local ladies that had also been through breast cancer and became an expert in my type of cancer. Right side, ductal carcinoma, 14mm, Grade 1, ER/PR positive HER2 negative initially told very slow growing, hasn't spread, lymph nodes look fine but I would have a sentinel node biopsy and was told by the consultant I was his 'easiest' conversation that day, don't think I'll ever get over the fact I was told I was an 'easy' conversation in the same breath I had been told I had cancer, CANCER FFS what the fuck is easy about that.

I didn't dwell on it however, after an initial meltdown I went home to tell my children, I had to do it, I knew I wouldn't cope with listening to my husband tell them it felt right for me to do it, my husband was shell shocked too. That conversation along with the excruciating wait for surgery/scan results has been by far the hardest part of this whole shit show.

It sounded like a straight forward diagnosis, I would be fine, wouldn't I? Curveball - positive lymph node, how the hell has this 'tiny, slow growing' bit of evil travelled already, grade 1 right..!! This is the unpredictability of cancer so further surgery it was, full axillary clearance with a lifetime risk of lymphedema and full body and bone scans, not entirely sure what I was more scared of, what if the cancer has spread, it's already proved it can travel....

Surgery went well with 'one small blip' my poor battered tit had now been burnt by the diathermy tool used to open the skin, manufacturing fault, really..!! What the actual fuck..!! So 3 burns to add to the scarring and no lymph nodes to fight any potential infection....shit, oh and a drain to drag around for 10 days, grim. However in the grand scheme of things, surgery has saved my life so I will embrace these scars along with the others and remain eternally grateful to my surgeon who was probably more upset than me.

Results - no further positive lymph nodes so given the all clear 1st December 2022 the only dark cloud, my surgeons words, is a 4mm lung nodule found during the CT and a hotspot on my hip found during the bone scan, I can't let these blips take over my life though.

Next stop Oncotype testing to see if I'd benefit from chemo, then radiotherapy and 10 years of anti hormone treatment. I know Chemo is absolutely the toughest treatment however I must admit I was surprised at how tough radiotherapy was, I didn't get the fatigue experienced by so many but man the burning boob that lasted for weeks was something else, and the permanent internal damage means my right side is still so tender plus cording is another delight that I wasn't prepared for. All minor ailments when you consider the alternative though, keep taking the positives.

Fast forward to today, no chemo and another 4 scans down the line I've been signed off from any more bone scans putting the hotspot down to benign arthritic changes and a stable lung nodule that could be anything, scarring, covid etc.. but will be scanned again in a years time.

So following my first clear annual mammogram I'm to just go live my life, I'm doing my best but the fear of recurrence is real.

In May this year I started volunteering with Breast Cancer Now and deliver public health talks to raise awareness, I'm also supporting a new 'Here for you' project too. I LOVE it and have found it really helps me, I know some people just want to pop their story in a box, close the lid and leave it there, and that's absolutely fine, but I need to be open, I need to talk about it, even had my 2 mins of fame on the ITV news, because believe it or not I've taken the positives from a negative situation.

I want to raise awareness, raise money and support others that find themselves faced with the reality of breast cancer.

This quote is one I really relate to - "The final stage of healing is using what happens to you to help other people" - Gloria Steinem

PHILIP ALDERSON

Lisa Alford - @ljalford71

TABBY LUXMOORE-STYLES

@tabbylstyles

Audio: @clemencybh : Another year of wonder @jackcullenmusic : Don't you Worry

"Oh Well.. Life's Shit And Then You Die" (My Granny's Response To Any Complaints..) Hopefully That Made You Grin Not Despair!

Aged 29, diagnosed with breast cancer on the left side. ER+ PR+ Have had lumpectomy, sentinel lymph node removal, 2 weeks of radiotherapy, 2 years hormonal treatment of tamoxifen daily pills, and self-administered Zoladex injections every 28 days (out of 5 years prescribed). Large amount of side effect management. Treated at Royal Marsden Fulham. Supported by @breastcancernow @maggiescentres @futuredreamscharity @royalmarsden

Context In Cancer Is Important

Everyone is different, every single persons cancer is different, how the medication affects each of us is different and what someone wants out of life will be different.

Items I will ALWAYS have with me

1. Hair clip (for hot flushes)

2. Bottle of water easily accessible

3. Scarf (for chills, and an impromptu eye mask when having a time out)

..and the enjoyable extras:

4. M&S Oven Roasted mixed nuts (for snacks)

5. Soft shoes (for sore joints and sensitive Achilles tendon)

6. Waterproof coat (not umbrella - sometimes difficult holding up an umbrella for a long period of time, esp if I have backpack on)

7. Cuddles (just because)

Couldn't do it without

• Movement - @shona_vertue

• Music - @clemencybh : Another year of wonder @jackcullenmusic Don't you Worry

• WhatsApp 'Broadcast Lists' - rather than making a group. It's the equivalent of a blog that you update, except you can share voicenotes and people can only respond

1:1, the list of names on the broadcast group is just for you to see/edit.

General Tips

1. Try to take the names of the doctors and nurses you're seeing and chase up referrals / important appointments, read the booklets, and keep a note of your symptoms and side effects to refer to- it's hard when you're on treatment to remember how you felt retrospectively.

2. Use the charities.

3. Be open to alternative therapies.

4. Trust your body and mind to come out the other side - you are doing brilliantly & you will be ok.

My 20%

I wrote a story on the theme of resilience for @seanchoiche which depicts some of my journey, and experience. Please note, everyone's experience is different and I know I am very fortunate in many ways to have had the option of these hardships & subsequent coping strategies- not a luxury that is afforded to everyone. Full video on Vimeo / link in my Instagram bio.

"So I've been having issues with a guy at work for the last year or so, let's call him Brian Jugs. It all started September 2021, and quite frankly I'm pretty happy to call him out as a complete prick.

How can I describe him to you? Well, if all the people on Hinge right now were like Brian, you'd be booking an urgent appointment to get your eggs frozen. And I did.

The big fall out from all this was not just my hair (I was left with trauma induced alopecia).

After any traumatic experience - therapy is the only option. And Brian is the sort of guy who'll get you on a fast track for not one, but three NHS therapists.

As these therapists have related to me, there are always lessons to be learnt from the worst characters that enter your life.

And when things looked pretty dia I realised I kept prioritising these values - perspective, thoughtfulness, and playfulness.

Now by this stage you're all probably thinking that Brian must be a real piece of work - so let me give you a bit more context on Mr Jugs.

A day before starting my very exciting new job, I was feeling myself up - ...as you do.... - And I found a lump, I went to have it tested and they told me there and then "I'm so sorry, it's cancer in your breast." I was on my own, thanks covid, at the hospital diagnostic centre, and the doctor just kept apologising, "I'm so sorry I'm really sorry". And I just kept saying "It's fine .. it's fine" with a sympathetic shrug.

This is how I first met the person we now call Brian Jugs. And I remember commenting on how great it is to be wearing masks in fact, because they're super absorbent for tears - that were just gently making their way down from my eyes.

I should also say at this stage the *reason* I checked, lying in bed on a Sunday morning was having seen a friends post on Instagram reminding people to have a feel - and it was during this "inventory" check that I actually found the lump.

So what did Brian teach me? Well of course he has been teaching me resilience.

Did I tell anyone? Yes. Pretty much anyone who'll listen. This here is no exception.

The path of least resistance, for me, is to be very open about it and ultimately there are obvious perks too (and I'm not just talking about my still excellent boobs!). I also found myself typing 'cancer discounts for hotels' into Google in November. (And I say that as if I've done it once, I've done it a few times - ok at least 40 times, they're some good deals out there) to any cancer muggles it's called playing the c-card (a brilliant initiative set up by Michelle Walder.)

And my cool points have gone through . the . roof! I got given 4 tattoos, thanks to radiotherapy (ps. there is an apt quote from TV show Friends: it's a tattoo of the earth as seen from a great great distance).. and what with all the Zoladex injections I'm still self-administering every month I can promise you I've never felt so badass.

In all honesty for every bad thing , there *was* a funny anecdote or heart warming moment, and my way of rationalising and keeping perspective was to always come back to what is ACTUALLY impacting me here - I'll give you 2 examples:

I was injecting myself everyday (pre egg harvest, what is that phrase?! the alternative is 'egg collection', bizarre again.. I just picture someone with a little basket coming round!). I can promise you though that pain of the injections & blood tests from *experienced* nurses is less than walking into the corner of a table or stubbing your toe. Psychologically, with the mention of "You're going to feel a small prick" (..definitely a joke in there somewhere…) you learn to catalogue different types of pain, and in reality on the pain scale a surprise stubbing of your toe is worse.

Second example of using perspective to tackle a tricky situation was during my Radiotherapy- I called it my mini meditation, reason being to get technical, cancer was on my left side which is the same side as the heart and radiotherapy causes scarring, which is fine on the lung (you have 2 of those) but not so fine on the heart (only 1) - so in order to avoid the beams going through my heart I had to do what's called a 'breath hold' which does what it says on the tin. I had to hold my breath for 20 seconds and the act of my lungs expanding would push my breast up and heart down away from the beams. Fascinating, in my opinion, but the best thing that came out of this radiotherapy experience was realising that really, all I was doing was lying still while a cool space age machine moved around me with these robotic arms, you can't feel anything happening and I just had to lie there and do 10 minutes of deep breathing exercises. I was able to embrace this and dial up the 'mini-meditation rhetoric' which in turn kept me calm - and I hate to say it, because it sounds weird, but it became an enjoyable part of my day.

So bringing us up to now, I'm still working through a reversible 'medically induced' Menopause started at 29, now I'm 31 - and yes the side effects just plain suck. But I *do* have love bursting at the seams in my life: my friends, family, therapists, an income, roof over my head, shoes on my feet - the cancer has been a *vehicle* for lovely things to be said and thoughtful gestures to be made. And basically my name in lights by standing up here telling this story!

But seriously - I am still categorically in the top 0.01% of the luckiest people on this planet, especially when you consider I can just waltz on in to a medical shop (pharmacy) to pick up life saving medicine every month, for FREE, so yes I feel pretty lucky.

Ive often been told - 'I don't know how you do it', and been asked 'do you feel enlightened?'

Well I can tell you ALL the answers - because I'm that clever (sarcastic eye roll) - Cancer has been a great excuse to get up here and have a play on my metaphorical trumpet.

I came to the conclusion that in my case, it was not the cancer diagnosis itself that's life changing, it's that with a change in circumstances you're also offered a choice, do you *want* to make this a life-changing event? And by that logic, that's something we all could choose to create any day of the week.

One thing has become clear with regards resilience - It's not some big clever, calculated approach to life.

Resilience seems to me to be both simple, and simply a sum of its parts.

This is the final section and congratulations to you for your resilience in sticking with me on this!

What I'm about to share with you is literally what the doctor ordered - and we know this stuff, it's not going to blow your socks off.

But if I explain... imagine your energy levels as a percentage % - so for me, still on treatment, I'm now operating (on a good day) at about 60%, on a bad day I could be 30/40%. Now that 20% difference is what these simple actions impact.

They are small(ish) margins, and barely noticeable if you're cruising along at a normal healthy 90/80% and then drop down to 60%.

So what are these simple, but ultimately life changing things that bolster that 20%:

1. do something you enjoy (this evening is a good start)

2. watch a comedy sketch everyday to ensure laughter (sounds lame but if you're not digging the day, then amusing YouTube scroll holes are good for you)

3. take time to immerse yourself in nature (this does not mean a luxury retreat, nature literally surrounds us, it's just out there, and free)

4. feel the fresh air on your face and breathe it in like that vicks commercial

5. make room for fun & games (whatever this means to you) - recently been painting at home and table football in the office for me

6. lie down on the floor curled up with your eyes closed and embrace the quiet / lack of stimuli

7. listen to music

8. stretch

9. sing (as close to someone's face as possible)

10. look at old photos/messages/think happy thoughts that make you smile

11. And my personal favourite, actually LOOK at strangers and give the awkward non threatening greeting of a small grin as you walk past

12. drop your shoulders

13. Eyes up

14. find something to be proud of

The *issue* with all these seemingly cliched and too good to be true, boring pieces of advice, is that we dismiss it as unimportant.. until we need it. That 20% is more valuable to me now than ever before, it makes a very real difference.

So now you have the full picture of where I'm coming from - sorry to anyone actually called Brian - we can rename him Brian the legend.

I have learnt to find perspective in a tricky moment, thoughtfulness is where I see the beauty of human connections come to life, and playfulness because in the words of Flanagan & Allen (my chosen song to sing along to, loudly, in someone's face):

"are you having fun? what you getting out of living? Are you getting any loving? Are you having any laughter? If other people do so can you. You ain't gonna live forever - what good is what you've got if you're not having any fun?"

PHILIP ALDERSON

Big hugs, you got this x

Tabby Luxmoore-styles - @tabbylstyles

CLAIRE MINIDRIVER

@cjbarden72

Don't rush your recovery and always use a heart shaped pillow after surgery!!

Claire Minidriver - @cjbarden72

PHILIP ALDERSON

JO KNIGHT

@tit_less_wonder

B is for Believe. As you navigate your way through appointments and treatment, never give up, never give in. It will be a rollercoaster of emotions but believing and having a positive outlook really does help.

R is for Rest, your body will need it, listen to it, don't push yourself too hard, sleep when you can (even if it's a 20 minute power nap!) you need your strength and energy. The housework can wait!

E is for Eating! Try to consume a healthy and balanced diet but at times during treatment you may only fancy certain foods (mine bizarrely was a pot noodle!!) eating something is better than nothing.

A is for Ask for help, don't suffer in silence. It's easy to hide away and not want to bother or trouble anyone and some days it's ok to do that! If family of friends offer help then take them up on it; picking up children from school, doing the ironing, cooking you dinner, doing your shopping. These little gestures can really help.

S is for Scanxeity....yes it's a thing!! Know that's it's normal to feel like that , try to keep yourself distracted, plan a treat for after your appointment- something to look forward to. Writing down how you're feeling can help sometimes.

T is for Take Notes, during appointment. There will be lots of words and terminology which will boggle your mind, some you may or may not remember. The OWise App is an excellent tool to use, it's s bit like an electronic diary, you can save all your appointments, add notes, record discussions and much more.

C is for Chemotherapy, something none of us ever want to go through but we don't have a choice. Just remember we are all different, we all react differently to treatment.Take each day at a time.

A is for Advocate for yourself, if something doesn't feel right or you maybe don't agree with something then challenge it, ask questions. You know your body best.

N is for Never google shit, the first rule of cancer club!

C is for Cold Capping/scalp cooling, this can help with hair loss. Ask your team questions, it's not for everyone and only effective with certain chemotherapy drugs but should be made available for you if your hospital offers it.

E is for Exercise or movement as I like to refer to it, the word exercise can fill some of us with fear!!! Try to keep your body moving during treatment, not always possible, but when you can, move that body, even if it's a 5 minute walk around the garden.

R is for Recovery. Life after cancer can be tough, take the time you need and be kind to yourself.

Jo Knight - @tit_less_wonder

PHIL ALDERSON

@philaldo

Audio: Baz Luhrmann - Sunscreen

Dear Cancer

We only met briefly in 2016, but what an impact you made.

You wanted to riddle my body with tumours.
You wanted to kill my organs.
You wanted me to worry.
You wanted me to be scared.
But things didn't go your way.

Instead, I was taken to a calm place with smiles, happiness, support, inspiring fighters and unique human spirit.

When I found you, I didn't know what you were - an innocent lump behind my left nipple. But I'd been training myself all my life for that very day. To take action without fear of the consequences, so I went to the doctors and got it checked out.

I could have ignored you.

I could have reacted slowly.

I could have been brushed aside by the doctors.

I could have needed more treatment.

I could have had PTSD.

I could have healed poorly.

In reality, everything that could have gone wrong, DIDN'T.

Ok, so I've lost a nipple, meh! I wasn't using it, and it was painful for a few months, medication side effects haven't been great, but every time I've felt sorry for myself, someone new would enter my life to remind me things could be a hell of a lot worse than they actually are. The universe helped me out a lot and still does to this day. She is a better friend than you.

All you took from me was 32 grams of tissue, and now I'm going to take everything I can from life that's possible, all because of you.

You're my excuse, my lottery ticket to make life better for myself and the people around me.

So far, because of you, I've met new people, made new friends, visited new places, and had experiences I could have never dreamed of. I've stood on skyscrapers, climbed mountains, been interviewed by journalists, appeared in newspapers and podcasts, met celebrities, learnt to dance, danced for a world champion judge, modelled for famous photographers and raised thousands for charity.

I'm determined to use you as a positive thing, the

opposite of what you wanted.

I've used you as a sign that I need to let go, say yes more and open my heart.

So I enjoy sitting in the sun and walking in nature, and I'm grateful to be able to do those simple things.

I'm going to 'live each day like it's my last', but what does that look like. In simple terms, it's doing things that you want to do instead of what is expected. Within reason, of course, for example, no bank heists.

Now I use you as my excuse to do everything I want to do. Don't be confused. It's still a rollercoaster, but it's a rollercoaster where I choose which car I'm sitting in, not you.

I'm not angry or resentful towards you, but seeing how you've treated other people is upsetting. You've not been as forgiving, and you've rampaged through my friends' bodies and left them mentally and physically beaten. For that, I can't forgive you.

Also, for terrorising and taking my father, I'll never forgive you.

I'm sure I would be a different person if you hadn't attempted to murder me. But, of course, I might still live in a world of scarcity and worry about doing anything for fear of...

'what would happen if I did....'

So Without Turning Into A Too Much Of A Cliche:-

Live your life to the fullest

Try to have no regrets

Talk to strangers

Upset a few people

Don't get upset by people

Be weird

Be yourself

Dance when you can

Wear sun lotion

Die with a few scars

Fuck the comfort zone

Memento Mori.

Remember, you will die of something, even if it's just old age, so choose to do something you love.

There are no rules. After all, who would have thought this 44-year-old man would have got breast cancer in the first place? Nevermind start modelling!

Phil Alderson - @philaldo

KARI BASTIAN

@bad_mammaries

A Warrior's Courage

In shadows cast by whispered fears,
A journey starts, soaked in silent tears.
A moment frozen, time suspended,
Breast cancer's grip, life upended.
A whispered word, a weight unseen,
A realm where strength and frailty convene.
The world transformed, colors fade,
In the stillness, a soul is laid.
A canvas painted with uncertainty,
Diagnosis etches its solemn decree.
Yet within the storm, a spirit stirs,
Resilience blooms, as courage transfers.
The echo of questions, a daunting maze,
Yet hope persists in myriad ways.

PHILIP ALDERSON

A warrior rises, adorned in grace,

Facing shadows, finding strength's embrace.

Through valleys deep, and peaks untold,

A tale of courage begins to unfold.

Each step a testament, a triumph sung,

In the symphony of battles, the heart is strung.

Whispers of support, a gentle breeze,

Caressing wounds with healing ease.

Together we stand, a united force,

Against the tide, a resilient course.

In the labyrinth of fear and despair,

A flicker of hope, a flame to bear.

For in the crucible of the unknown,

A warrior's spirit steadily grown.

Though the journey may be steep,

Each heartbeat, a promise to keep.

In the tapestry of life, threads rearrange,

A testament to the strength of change.

Kari Bastian - @bad_mammaries

GINA DAVIDSON

@ginalouisedavidson

"A Lot Of People Don't Understand Why I Have Come To This Decision To Go Flat On One Side. But They Haven't Felt Like I Felt."

My name is Gina, I'm 53 years old and I live in the North of England. My wonderful husband and I have four children – two girls and two boys, they are my world. I was diagnosed with breast cancer in May 2022. I got called for my first routine mammogram at age 52; I got a letter which called me back for further tests because they had seen some suspicious things on one side. I hadn't felt a thing myself. The fact that I was 52 when I had my first mammogram shook me. Other women had one at 48. If I had had this done earlier, would I have needed a less major operation?

Operation after operation

I had a mastectomy, during which they took every bit of breast tissue, the nipple and the lymph nodes as well. My cancer was caught early, it hadn't spread through my lymph nodes so thankfully I didn't need any further treatment like radiotherapy – just hormone therapy. I opted for an immediate reconstruction using a muscle from my back, which was done at the time of the mastectomy. Two hours afterwards, I had a hematoma, so I had to go back into surgery for another five-hour operation. Since then I've had another surgery to increase the size of my breast and form a nipple. But I hate what it looks like, what it feels like and how it makes me feel. My surgeon sent me to counselling with a health psychologist and, as a result of this, he has agreed to remove my reconstructed breast. That final operation was planned for May, but it was cancelled because of covid-19. I am looking forward to getting the removal done so I can finally close that chapter of my life.

When you first get your diagnosis it's a whirlwind. I have never been ill, I have never been in the hospital, it was a complete shock. I was told all my options, which was to have a mastectomy and stay flat, to have an implant, to have the operation that I opted for or to have one where they use my belly fat. It's very difficult to make informed decisions when you're being told so much. I went for the one that uses my back muscle because the surgeon who was doing it was a pioneer in that operation, and therefore was trying to sell it to me. "You're a prime candidate, it will be amazing, we'll just need one or maybe two operations". Here I am, down the line, I've had three operations and they said I would need three more. And I'm only a B cup, I'm not a busty woman! A lot of people don't understand why I have come to this decision to go flat on one side. But they haven't felt like I felt. It has been very hard, mentally and physically. It has been a tough decision, but it is the decision that is right for me.

Going Flat

The best advice that I would give my earlier self is to speak to other women that have had breast cancer. You have to talk to your surgeon, and you have to talk to the breast care nurses (who are all amazing), but the women I spoke to that have had breast cancer were the most helpful. Some other advice is to take time to make your decision. I know that when you get a diagnosis of cancer there isn't much time, you have to have the operation straight away. But you can have the mastectomy, and once you have healed physically and mentally, then you can think with a clear head about what procedure you would like to go ahead with. I'm having my breast taken away now, but if I change my mind in four years, five years, however many years, they can put an implant in or they can do another reconstructive surgery. That door is never closed to you, it's there for the rest of your life.

Actually, I would like to have my other breast removed too, but they say no because they don't want to operate on a piece of me that is healthy. This worries me, because in the back of my head there is still the chance of me getting breast cancer again. I found out only this week that 30% of women who have breast cancer get secondary cancer at a later stage. That's a high percentage and secondary breast cancer is most often incurable once it gets to your liver and to your bones.

As for life with one breast, I think I will like having the option to wear a prosthetic bra for special occasions. But I've never liked wearing tight clothes anyhow, so I feel I can hide my chest quite easily. And sometimes I just can't be bothered. You know, I'm a 53 year old woman, I have four children, I don't need to worry about how I look and how my body looks. I know my husband loves me anyway!

Time And Talking

I have lost a lot of body confidence. For a long while, I wouldn't undress in front of my husband, and I wouldn't let him touch me at all. I thought my body was grotesque. I used to be a very outdoorsy woman, sailing yachts, hill walking, doing all sorts of things. It might not be forever, but at the moment I feel like I couldn't do anything like that anymore. New situations, meeting new people, going out of my house is still a struggle. I have been through the mill with depression from my diagnosis, and it was really strange because I thought it was my husband who had depression. I rang his sister to talk it through and she said "No Gina, it's you". We had a long chat and I broke down and I realized that it was me that had the depression. I was upsetting my husband, that's why he was not himself. To admit that was really hard, so if people are out there to support people with that, that's so amazing. Time is a great healer; time and talking. Through the support of my family and social media – I can't believe the support I got through social media, it's incredible! – I am gaining more confidence. There is this whole community that I am listening and talking to, and I think that's why I was able to make the decision that I don't need that breast to be feminine, to be me.

Since I have been speaking to people about this online, I have been approached to be part of a documentary, I've had a few interviews and I do fundraising. The more things I can get involved in, the better. Something good has to come from me getting cancer; of course, it was an awful thing to go through, but even if I just inspire one person or help one person make the right decision for themselves then I am happy. That has really helped my own personal healing too. I don't want to forget about having breast cancer. It will always be in my life, and therefore I have to make it positive.

Family

I only have two of my four children living at home now, but when I first got my diagnosis I asked the other two to come home for the weekend so we could sit down and talk about it. They have looked after me all the way through. My husband had actually lost his job the month before my diagnosis. There are very few positives about losing your job, but the silver lining is that he was there with me the whole time.

My girls and I have a very open relationship, we talk about everything. I thought my boys wouldn't really want to talk about it, 'that's women's things', but they have and they still talk about it to me! They have surprised me, and they have been amazing.

Something I'm really looking forward to is getting matching tattoos with my two daughters. Once I've had my surgery and I'm healed we're going to get a tattoo done on our right breast. I've never wanted a tattoo but this is going to be very meaningful for all three of us. My daughter is going to draw the design, I don't want anything big, just a tiny little flower or something. I'm actually a bit scared of having a tattoo! But if I can get through what I went through, I can deal with a little tattoo, right?

Gina Davidson - @ginalouisedavidson

KARLA CORNWALL

@karlas_lifes4living

Live Life To The Fullest

Every person has their own story of what they've experienced with cancer.

I wanted to put a positive spin on my cancer diagnosis and give hope that in sadness and darkness there is also light!

I put this poem together in just 10 minutes, it just seemed to flow.

❖ ❖ ❖

Cancer, a rollercoaster ride you don't expect to be on,

You don't realize how much your tested and how you can be strong,

Up, down, round and round, emotional, sad, it's hard to keep your feet on the ground.

But with all I've been through, my family and friends too,

Ive been on a journey of self love, self discovery

Im finally happy just being me.

Through the ups and the downs Ive found less time to frown,

I often think myself holy cow

But boy do i see life so differently now.

It's the smaller simple things I took for granted,

I consider myself now I've just been replanted, time to water myself and grow,

To enjoy the little things in life but with a pace more slow.

With a love for walking and talking thanks to the Coppafeel trek,

Ive made new friends for life and made memories I'll never forget.

And now I make the most of each day,

Living and loving in every way.

Stop and breathe and take each moment at a time,

You will get through the tough it's definitely a climb.

Live life to the fullest and smile,

We're only here once it's not a trial ♥

#coppafeel   #poem   #poetry   #lifeaftercancer #lifeisforliving

Karla Cornwall - @karlas_lifes4living

LISA FLEMING

@living_as_lisa

Audio: Brave (Sara Bareilles)

Dying To Live

Our world turned upside down, a diagnosis so severe.

At the young age of 33, metastatic breast cancer brings tears of fear.

Incurable, they say, 6 months at the most, a road to hell lies ahead.

But with love, support and friendship, you won't be easily led.

Hair loss follows, a visible and mentally challenging sign of 'the fight'.

Yet your inner beauty shines, radiating light

Chemotherapy courses through your veins so strong

People rally telling you that your 'doing so well fighting the battle' it's to hard to tell them the truth and explain that they are wrong.

A few months down the line the first brain surgery looms,

a daunting step to take

But still within you lies a strength that no matter what you endure it won't break.

Fear may grip your heart, casting shadows of doubt

But know you're not alone, as a community, you have clout

Radiation the next step on this journey you face, with each burn you face with treatment, you dig deep and show that strength across your face.

Your tribe stands by you, a pillar of support and care. It takes courage to step away and move on from those who aren't there.

Rebuilding your life, piece by piece, day by day

Finding solace in small victories along the way

Through the ups and downs, you'll rise above

With the unwavering support of those you love

Incurable, yes, but hope still burns bright

A inner spirit unyielding, a beacon of light

Together, we stand, side by side. Rebuilding, living life in the best way we can whilst taking our fate in our stride.

Lisa xx

Lisa Fleming - @living_as_lisa

MARTINA

@heartsnstarsbymarticlare

When I meet Phil @philaldo in person, we spoke about our own personal experience of breast cancer.

Phil said his advice is don't Google. I said weirdly enough I was the complete opposite.

I just wanted to be prepared for what they might thrown at me next! I'm not sure if it helped or not, but it made me feel like I wasn't going to get any more shock news and I had a rough idea what my consultant was talking about when we meet (not all medical terms obviously)

I felt I was "prepared".

At each stage for me, I Googled lumpectomy, Hickman lines, chemotherapy, radiotherapy Tamoxifen, menopause thanks to chemo, the lot!

This somehow made me feel a little bit in control, I know that sounds crazy because this is cancer we are talking about, but it worked for me!

Basically I'm saying do what is right for YOU and

your personality! Google, don't Google, read about your condition or don't read anything, listen to advise and follow it or not.

Everyone's experience is different. You choose how to handle it.

There is no one size fits all for people going through this horrible disease.

Take care.

Martina, Glasgow. Breast cancer survivor since 2006. Diagnosed at age 43 with Grade 2 HER2- ER+

#breastcancernow   #breastcancerawarnessmonth
#coppafeel   #fuckcancer   #cancersupport
#breastcancersurvivor #philaldobook

Martina - @heartsnstarsbymarticlare

SAM CUMMINS

@sam_cummins77

Share Your Story

This October was my first Breast Cancer Awareness Month with breast cancer. Secondary breast cancer. And I was surprised by things I saw from others in the community.

There is a negative side to BCAM, when I can see only positive.

People seem to not like that it's pink. It's just a colour that's assigned, as Alzheimer's is purple, and mental health is green.

Does it matter? Should we change it? In truth, when you hear breast cancer, you think pink. Probably because we've seen the campaign for so long. It's good there's an association, because it raises awareness.

Yes, we're all aware of breast cancer, but are we fully aware? I can only answer for me, and I can say with certainty, no. No, I don't know all there is to know. Before I had BC, I had no idea there were different types. Or different treatments. I didn't know secondary breast cancer was a thing, or that you could be diagnosed without having had primary. I didn't even know about the term primary!

Primary -

1. of chief importance; principal.

2. earliest in time or order.

Opposite - secondary

What does this mean?! Does it mean primary is better? More important? It can also mean earliest, but I didn't have primary so how do I have SBC?

We have BCAM every year and still don't know these things. Which shows that we need more awareness.

Every month should be BCAM, and in my world, it is. Because I share my story, or at least some information, EVERY month. It's clear the campaign can't reach everyone. When people share their stories, it brings life to the facts and figures. It shows that you can never be too young, that you can be a man, that it's found in different ways. When people share their stories, others see, and become aware.

I have found a community of amazing people, who are strong, resilient, positive and inspiring. @sparkling_mandy is one of the smiliest, most positive, vibrant people. She loves a selfie, and lit her whole house purple for SBC Awareness Day, complete with giant light up boobs! What a lady! I never would have met her without SBC.

Breast cancer is not pink and fluffy - I'm not sure who ever said it was! - but if turning the world pink for one month helps even a few people learn something new, and seek help, then light it up!! Make the bloody world pink!

Sam Cummins - @sam_cummins77

PHILIP ALDERSON

PREETI

@thebigcccoach

Like most people who have been diagnosed with Cancer it was a complete shock to me. Dealing with the diagnosis, informing loved ones, going through treatment was hard, but I got through pretty much unscathed.

For me the problems set in once treatment had finished. I had always been fierce in my approach to life and had approached my numerous health and life challenges like a warrior. That was until I was faced with Breast Cancer. Even though physically I had recovered well and quite quickly, mentally I was a wreck.

Leaving the Consultants office with the all-clear I had had a fleeting wave of relief, before the dread set in. A tsunami of questions plagued me, what was next? how do I get back to normal? why wasn't I jumping for joy? and as the days passed, I fell into a slump.

My medical team had gone away, and my family and friends all returned to their normal lives, but I just couldn't go back to normal. I didn't know whether I couldn't or didn't want to. Getting out of bed was a struggle, I would spend the day in my night robe and have random episodes of bursting into tears. I felt alone, isolated and my anxiety was through the roof.

It got so bad that I gave up my job, I could not face going back and I didn't know why I felt so bad. It was like I was lost and grieving for a part of me that was gone. With time, slowly things started to get better, after darkness always comes light. It took some time but what helped me survive that slump were the following:

- Giving myself permission to be in this phase

- Allowing myself time to really feel my emotions and sit with them

- Having self-awareness about what I needed at that time

- Putting myself first and being kind to myself

- Letting go of people and things that drained my energy.

I found that these simple steps helped me deal with one of the most challenging phases of my life and I would encourage anyone who is facing breast cancer and feeling lost and at a loss to try these steps.

You will find your unique way to overcome this stage. I have managed to turn my life around since and really worked on my mindset and now I share my skills and knowledge with others facing their cancer journey. I found purpose through my pain and you can too.

Preeti - @thebigcccoach

JEANNIE

@jambeannie

Survival Advice

I was diagnosed with Secondary Breast Cancer in May 2019. I went from thinking I was healthy to finding out I had tumours in both breasts which had spread to my bones, an estimated life expectancy of 3-5 years.

It's difficult coming to terms with your own mortality, knowing your time is limited and the approaching devastation for your loved ones. The saying 'this too shall pass' just doesn't apply to me. I have to learn to live with this, to live well and not in fear. It's a big ask for anyone. I try hard to look after my mental health or else I can feel myself on a downward spiral. I'm quite a lively person and my little mind needs calming down. I have Indian head massages and I try to practice mindfulness and relaxation. It's not going to happen every day, but I do feel more able to cope when I've looked after my mind and encouraged peace.

I'm asking what do I want from my life? What and who makes me happy? Anything that makes me feel good I try and do as much as possible. I love being outdoors. And the sea, oh I love the sea, I try to get to a beach walk every so often. Pre-cancer I was very holiday driven. Always wanting special family moments abroad and searching for the next special trip. I still love to travel but now I know that the perfect moments are surrounding me, just being with those I love and feeling close. I appreciate everything more. Sounds dreamy but I must add this hasn't turned me into a magical fairy, I still moan about dirty plates not actually making it into the dishwasher (it's really not that hard) and who the hell keeps leaving all that toothpaste in the sink, but my perfect moments are here in the everyday.

Finding other patients in the same situation has been invaluable for me. When someone else knows exactly how you are feeling it's such a relief. Find your tribe, I found mine on social media. Family and friends, essentially people are love and I can really feel the support. Plus, I think I'm hilarious so people respond to my funny jokes. It's mainly sympathy 'likes' but who cares, makes me feel like a winner.

Obviously, there are some really dark moments when it feels so sad and overwhelming and I just need to cry and let it all out. Sometimes I know I'm on the edge so I don't watch or read anything that might start me off. I once watched a Disney film about a dog and sobbed, the dog hadn't even died I just thought it might. Damn you Disney. When I'm low I just try to have faith in myself, I know I can get through, I just have to let this sadness wash over me and I will recover to carry on again.

It's not always easy but there is still a wonderful life to be lived. And I am going to live it.

Jeannie - @jambeannie

CHANTEL CHANTILUKE

@supa.chan

Audio: Beyoncé - Church Girl

So You Have Cancer, What's Next?

My advice for making it through a breast cancer diagnosis is whatever your treatment plan, you will make it through thick and thin. The highs and the lows.

I was diagnosed with inflammatory breast cancer at 11 weeks pregnant and I genuinely did not know how I would make it to the end of my pregnancy, let alone, how would cancer treatment look like.

From being diagnosed, to starting chemo, having a baby, getting a mastectomy to now restarting chemo again due to the cancer spreading to the other breast, this has all been incredibly overwhelming! Doctors, surgeons, consultants all talking to me like the treatment will happen to me without giving it a second chance.

That's the thick of it. Feeling like you don't have a chance to process your emotions while the physical side of cancer takes its toll.

For everything I truly thought was hard, I have now overcome in some way. Making it through rounds of chemo all with varying degrees of how the symptoms affect me while pregnant. A 3 day induction process to give birth to my baby girl. Having a mastectomy while my daughter was 12 days old and recovering with her, my 20 month old son and my husband.

This cancer journey will be longer than I expected. In between all the appointments and treatments there has always been a time I have been able to lift my head up high, take a breath, and focus on the good times by celebrating the small wins.

That's when I can say I've made it through a thick time, when there is a glimmer of hope, when I can laugh again. I have family, friends and I'm part of a wonderful cancer community all of which give me hope and strength to carry on and to vent when I need to.

Find your circle of people, keep them close, through the highs and lows.

Oh and if you can, make a playlist on whatever platform you listen to music! I've found it helpful saving songs that stirred an emotion in whatever way and it's always nice to go back to it, like it's a musical journey for how far you have come! Music to cry to, dance along to the beat, something to have in the background while I sat in the chair for chemo, there is a song for everything!

Chantel aka supa.chan

Chantel Chantiluke - @supa.chan

NICOLA COLLINGS

@lifegonetitsup

Survival Tip

No matter what happens, never stop having fun and being silly! Life is for living! During a cancer diagnosis, and treatment, there will be lots of lows but seeing the positive (no matter how small) in every day will really push you through the hard times.

I have been heavily inspired by @lisa.acooper I first met Lisa on Instagram, but have since met her in person via a cancer group, and her spirit and laugh are infectious!! She makes me belly laugh and her ways of coping have been truly inspirational.

Nicola Collings - @lifegonetitsup

PHILIP ALDERSON

DR LIZ O'RIORDAN

@oriordanliz

I've thought long and hard about what advice I would give to anyone diagnosed with breast cancer

I've had it three times, and what I think now is very different to what I felt in the beginning, back in 2015

But @philaldo was very persuasive and is collecting all our words of wisdom for his book, so here we go…

Breast Cancer is just a plot twist in the story of your life

It's up to you what happens next

What you do with the life you have left

Go out there and make memories with the people you love

Don't let it define you

Dr Liz O'Riordan - @oriordanliz

PHILIP ALDERSON

CLAIRE WOOLGER

@sunglasses_in_the_rain

Audio: P!NK's music got me through.

Someone's Survival Guide @Philaldo

My entry would be these words & the poem I wrote to try and capture the change in perspective going through breast cancer (my second cancer aged 32 - possibly the result of being treated for one as a teenager) has prompted.

The first time round the cancer block as a teenager left me all the more determined to throw myself at pursuing a "normal" life. I had 17 years of wonderful cancer-free life before diagnosis of BC this year. It broke me.

I feel now that I have an 80-year-old's-head on a 32 year-old's shoulders, as much as I wouldn't have asked for this (who would?!) that sort of perspective at my age (hopefully with years to live) is a gift of sorts.

With the darkness of a cancer diagnosis - the light becomes all the brighter: from the phenomenal compassion of staff in the NHS, through to the unwavering support from family & friends, the gratitude I feel for the love that surrounds me is achingly beautiful in its power! Each person is another thread in a net that's stopped me slipping through the cracks. And awareness of/ gratitude for this is the only thing that outshouts The Fear.

Life is spectacularly precious in its fragility & accepting this is not a one off act. You've got to dare to live & after the life-destruction of a diagnosis, leaning into life is the greatest risk of them all! But there is no other way really.

Inspired by @oriordanliz & - ! & @donnaashworthwords - revealing the power of hope through poetry!

#philaldobook   #breastcancer   #teenagecancer #rhabdomyosarcoma   #breastcancerinmy30s   #nhs #poetry #poetrycommunity #voiceofcancerpatients

Claire Woolger - @sunglasses_in_the_rain

KARLINA LOUISE

@karlinalouise

Audio: Jhene Aiko - W.A.Y.S

You Have Gotta Loose Your Mind Just To Find Your Peace Of Mind

25 years old I found the lump.

26 years old I was diagnosed.

27 years old I'm cancer free.

I am 28 a week a week after xmas.

Life flies by so fast when you're fighting for your life & living with what seems like the grim reaper.

I don't think about my diagnosis as much as I think I should, my mind has been able to do this 'shut off' thing. Blessing or curse I'm not sure. Or maybe just a trauma response.

When I was first diagnosed I remember my consultant told me this one thing that my mind couldn't comprehend and that was "you'll learn how to live with it", at the time I was mortified like HOW?

But he couldn't be more right... I'm not sure how we're able to do but we do it.

What I wasn't prepared for was how many friends I'd loose throughout this.

But, I am so thankful that if cancer taught me anything it's it reveals who's really there for you and that includes family too - but also just how superhuman you are.

You go into the cancer world so scared and vulnerable.

You come out a completely different person, I PROMISE you.. you won't be the same.

All the little things that used to bother you pre cancer, won't bother you no more. For you have battled so hard, that peace is the only thing you crave.

We are not what happened to us!

I am not just surviving now, but thriving. I'm not broken, I am healing.

Don't loose hope, some days are tough, others days after better, stay off google, no two people are the same. Cancer is complex af.

Toxic positivity is a real thing. You're allowed to feel how you feel, whether that's angry, sad, resentful it's all relative.

And if you need a bit of encouragement please read this book - for we are the aftermath

Karlina Louise - @karlinalouise

GEMMA BRADBURY

@medical_menopause_empowerment

2019 My Life Felt Perfect And Then Towards The End Of The Year My Life Crumbled When My Relationship Ended, I Was Diagnosed With Breast Cancer And We Went Into Lockdown.

Through the pandemic I was lucky enough that none of my treatment was delayed but unlucky in that it also meant that I had to pull up my big girl pants and go to appointments by myself (apart from at the very start when my mum when came with me and held my hand).

From my very first operation I learnt how important it was to find people you can relate too and luckily for me I met 2 amazing women who were in the same shoes and had their lumpectomies the same day as me.

The worst part of the cancer process is the constant 2 week intervals where you wait for news and with these girls by my side I at least knew that they understood exactly how I felt. I found that initially I was ok but as the d-day approached I found it was so hard to even think straight knowing that soon I would understand exactly what I was facing.

On the day of my initial operation my surgeon mentioned the oncotype test which came as a massive blow as up to that point I was told it was caught early and I'd probably only need radiotherapy so knowing that chemotherapy would be a possibility floored me.

The breast care team and the Macmillan nurse were absolutely amazing and kept in regular touch with me and were so supportive even if sometimes all I did was cry down the phone.

As this was the start of lockdown and I was a newly single parent I was navigating a lot of this alone and didn't want to burden my family and friends with how I felt. With my daughters at home I used the opportunity to go sit in my youngest daughter's nursery and cry alone wondering how my life had actually come to this in such a short space of time. Hiding away to cry became my new normal and is something I still do to this day if I need a moment to collect myself.

Unfortunately the margins from my first operation were not clear which meant I had to go through another operation and this time completely by myself but the nurses at the hospital were amazing and kept me company and held my hand when I needed it.

Through the following radiotherapy appointments, treatments and then navigating first tamoxifen and then zoladex and letrozole I really leaned on the virtual friendships I had made and many a night was spent at my laptop pouring through Facebook posts and feeling the virtual love from all around the world.

Through my whole journey and to date now I've learn how important it is is to find your tribe, from the amazing women I met on my first operation to the Facebook groups and now through instagram I'm constantly humbled and amazed by the group of strong, powerful, real and kick ass women I have met. Unfortunately some people drift in and out of your lives but the bonds that I have now are so strong and I am forever grateful for these women!

Cancer is scary and a club that nobody wants to find themselves in, but through these dark moments we really do meet beacons of light and through this you suddenly don't feel so alone anymore!

Gemma Bradbury - @medical_menopause_empowerment

PHILIP ALDERSON

CHARLOTTE ROSE

@charlottexrose

Having it made me stronger, that's for sure,

A journey of resilience, a battle to endure.

Through the darkest nights, I found inner light,

A spirit unwavering, shining ever so bright.

In the face of adversity, I stood tall,

Fighting with every ounce of strength, giving it my all.

It tried to break me, but I refused to fall,

A warrior emerged, standing proud and standing tall.

Through the pain and tears, I discovered my might,

A newfound courage, like a beacon in the night.

I faced my fears head-on, embraced the unknown,

Finding strength within myself that had previously been unknown.

It taught me lessons, profound and deep,

To cherish every moment, to treasure and keep.

It showed me the power of love and support,

From family and friends, a lifeline of comfort.

So though the journey was tough, I emerged with grace,

A survivor, a fighter, with a smile on my face.

It made me stronger, it tested my core,

But I rose above it all, and I'll keep fighting forevermore.

By Charlotte Rose

Charlotte Rose - @charlottexrose

NIKKI J

@spinalnikki

What Would I Tell Future Breast Cancer Patients?

Find your tribe! Find those on the same journey as you, albeit might be a different carriage. Support in the Cancer Community is amazing.

Say yes to new opportunities.

Find joy in everyday things. Push your boundaries a little, you never know what you can achieve!

Spend time with your family & friends, because they are also riding the storm, but in a lifeboat! Make memories and time.

For those in the Secondary breast cancer community also means that when you find your tribe, you also will lose alot of your tribe.

This is the reality.

However, it should not stop you from meeting the most amazing, beautiful, kindest souls to ever meet.

It's a club no one wants to be in, but if you are it's a

club where you meet the most amazing and inspiring individuals!

I have met many individuals, attended events and tried new experiences, that would not have occurred if I hadn't been dealt the cancer card.

But you shouldn't have to have a life limiting illness or disease to make you wake up and see the beauty that is all around you and to try new experiences and do what brings you joy.

And whatever you do........

DO NOT ASK DR GOOGLE!!!!!!

#philaldo #philaldobook
#livingwithmetastaticbreastcancer #findyourtribe
#storiesofhope #spinalnikki #fightingtobeheard
#findthejoy #bethebestyoucanbe

nikki j - @spinalnikki

STEPHANIE ARNOLD

@nowpanicandfreakout

My Best Advice To Anyone Facing Cancer Is To Set Up A Support Network. Family, Friends Or Neighbours, You Shouldn't Go It Alone.

Join a support group for your type of cancer, preferably in person because you bond so quickly.

Get a binder to stay organised.

If possible, do stretches, walking,

and lastly, be patient with yourself, you will not be able to carry on as usual.

Recovery will take much longer than you expect. You will meet many people while in your cancer journey who can provide you with encouragement, love, support and camaraderie.

Stephanie Arnold - @nowpanicandfreakout

PHILIP ALDERSON

CINDY BEEHLER

@byebitch_ibc

My Darkest Days

I never thought it would happen
Then I got the call
My life has changed forever
I slowly start to fall
Survival mode is all I know
I'm fighting to persevere
I don't know any different
My life feels betwixt and between
Will my daughter grow up without me?
Will I miss her life?
Her face is all I need to see
To start to fight this war
My body has betrayed me
Yet she fights to stay alive

The pain I feel from chemo

It keeps me up at night

Some days I can hardly walk

The pain can run so deep

How do I distract myself?

From going insane?

All the doctors, treatment, hospital stays

All the drugs, radiation and pain

They get to live rent-free

Directly in my brain

I get lost in a book

Or my favourite comfort show

Put on my favourite music

Because it is then that I know

I don't have to have those thoughts

The ones that make me cry

I get to have some time

To think that I can fly

I have my support system

Plus all of my new friends

The cancer community was there for me

When no one understood

This new place is not somewhere

That I ever wanted to be

But the one thing I have kept

And will hold forever dear

Are all the people who have

Helped me live with this fear

Cindy Beehler - @byebitch_ibc

PHILIP ALDERSON

VANESSA THACKER

@breast_intentions_

My Story Is My Story That's My Advice

Try not to compare to others definitely don't google things ..

My Story

My cancer came out of the blue whist away with work I found a lump large one in my right breast but at the time I wasn't concerned or worried I had previously had bad car accident damaged my right shoulder chest & collarbone so assumed it was that, even when a week later I went to my doctors they wasn't concerned either due to past trauma they too assumed it was nothing so when your doctor says that you think yes I'm ok.

But there's always but I got referred to breast clinic less then week later to just check things out even at this point I was convinced it was nothing .

But that day sits in my memory more so people were having scans coming out getting changed but I had been in for my scan already but was told not to change to sit in this corner it's crazy things you remember 6 chairs in l shape just me my carrier bag of clothing in my hospital gown

My partner was in waiting room and I texted to say I'm sure nurses are looking at me weird he was don't be silly you been in there ages that's all ..

but I remember my mind setting changing somethings wrong ?!

Something was wrong I got sent to have multiple mammograms which was strange then ultra sound at this point I knew by the weird conversations the nurses were having with me very random ones they were trying to distract me tv screens brightened up the dark small room but the movie for today was my boobies clear to see that the right one inside looked very different to my left panic set in

Six biopsies later very sore boob & the kind of emotion I couldn't control I broke down they even let me walk out to crowded waiting area to see my partner in my gown blood & all with tears streaming down my face they didn't say it was cancer but I knew ..

we had to go and see consultant the one at the start of the appointment who said you will have scans & go home if there's no issues if you come back to me then that's different story

I even joked I'm back

I was direct after losing my dad so quickly to cancer I had to be

I know you can't tell me but is it cancer

The answer I was imagining was let's wait

But again there's another but ...

He just came out with it I've worked in breast care for many years I retired come back to help after Covid but you have cancer Vanessa & I saw this sadness in his eyes he touched my hand said I hoped I wouldn't see you again but here we are then starting going on about survival rates finding cancer early but I didn't hear much of that I needed to get out of that room now the air had left my body for me that was the worst time of my life

We skip good few months varied medications Covid delayed surgery's being told my cancer wasn't aggressive but invasive

to me that part was just a blur way I explain it now it felt like I wasn't me I was just playing a part in someone else's life .

My surgery was over 16 hours brutal but surprising I woke up better then I thought

Right sided skin saving mastectomy with skin flap reconstruction breast bone reconstruction lymph node removal

It's crazy to think now year on that was me

Chemo for me was my worst thought was always told that it's possible in my head if I looked like me on the outside then I could take on the world I could still be me regardless & I was extremely lucky I hate that word lucky were not lucky but you get what I mean ..

My breast bone & lymph nodes come back clear told that

chemo wasn't going to be option

By this time with medication stress my hair was thinning out I think it was like my body preparing for my worst which to me was always chemo losing my identity little did I know that my mindset would change my identity changed anyway & I was grateful I was here regardless of what I looked like to me if the world saw me sick I was sick but if I could look well I was well crazy thought process as I wasn't well but kept me fighting ..

I thought after being diagnosed surgery over cancer gone life would be easy but I think I've found life after cancer so much harder then I ever imagined the cancers gone but your left with a person that isn't you although it's great life we navigate the meds the ever changing ones

Were not the same person and a saying I still say to this day

WERE STRONGER THAN WE EVER BELIEVED

Vanessa Thacker - @breast_intentions_

LAURA MCGOWAN

@abcdfucancer

After loosing my 41 year old sister to Sarcoma cancer in 2018 a mere 5 months later - age 28 - I was diagnosed with primary breast cancer, I thought I was lucky & had a great escape after only needing a lumpectomy, radiotherapy & hormone therapy.

Fast forward to 2022 my 42 year old brother was diagnosed & continues to battle stage 4 colon cancer.

Shortly after his diagnosis I knew I didn't feel right but couldn't work out exactly why. After several trips to GPs, breast clinic, gynecology & A&E over the space of about 10 months... In April 2023 - age 33 - I was diagnosed with stage 4 breast cancer spread to my bones and liver.

My survival advice would be;

- Take time to grieve (whither that's someone you have lost, have a loved one diagnosed or just the loss of the pre-cancer version of yourself, or in my case - all of the above!)

- Decide how you are going to face this, but most importantly, work out how you can help yourself & make one small change at a time until they become habit.

- Allow yourself down days & wobbles, we are only human after all, but never forget to pick yourself back up!!

- Accept help if it's offered - it's not weak!

- Speak to someone - but not a friend or family member - a therapist, psychologist or councillor... I promise it is helpful

- Fill your head with positivity & avoid comparing your diagnosis with others, no 2 of us are the same!

And finally...

- Take one day, one hour, one step at a time. Do not look too far into the future as no one can predict this, no matter the circumstances!

Life is not over, it may well be just begining with your eyes wide open to what's important ♥

Sending lots of positive vibes to anyone who needs it!

Laura McGowan - @abcdfucancer

AIMÉE

@onestrongday

My Story Is A Tale Of Extreme Resilience

For the last 4 years I've sustained several hits from recurrent clots, anaphylaxis and of course breast cancer, all while navigating parenting two young neurodivergent children. My mum also passed away due to breast cancer, while undergoing chemo myself.

My tips go as follows:

Have a hospital bag prepped. Change of clothes, snacks and entertainment are a must. Mine has a puzzle book and chamomile tea bags.

Find your people / support network. They are the ones who will help get you through.

Comfort. Wrap yourself in blankets. Take that bath. Find your calming strategies. In hospital I use grounding techniques and mindfulness.

Have something to look forward to. A meal, a trip out, a holiday. Gives you something to focus on.

Give yourself space to feel however you feel. Counselling also helps. I'd also recommend @mindcharity for support.

I'm still standing and grateful to be here ♥ hope this helps someone who is going through a tough time.

#philaldobook @philaldo

So many people inspire me so it's hard to select one!

@rachel_x_ann

@lovinglife.with.wendy

@emmasknackeredknockers

Aimée - @onestrongday

PATTI CAREY

@pfastycarey

Audio: "Don't Give Up on Me" by Andy Grammer

Even If You Stumble, You Are Still Moving Forward

This is my go to quote when life's difficulties arise. Hearing the words, you've got cancer multiple times, twice with breast cancer (2002 & 2017) and with a chronic leukemia (2017), will make you feel like you are free-falling. When you fall, you have to learn how to get back up and move on. That is the lesson learned on my multiple cancer journey.

Hearing the word cancer frightened me in 2002, not so much in 2017. Now the attitude is, this is just a stumble on life's road and for me that makes it a little easier to move forward.

In 2002 at the age of 43, I was diagnosed Stage 1 ER+, PR +Her2+ invasive ductal carcinoma included a lumpectomy, radiation, chemo, Tamoxifen & Arimidex. At that time, I had another issue going, my dad was in hospice for prostate cancer & passed away.

One of the best proactive decisions I have made in my cancer journey was genetic testing. I have the CHEK2+, which increase my odds of getting a second breast cancer. Did aggressive screening alternating every 6 months between mammogram and a breast MRI until 2017.

Life was good and my journey back to the "new" normal was moving forward, then came 2017. Wound up being diagnosed with double whammy a 2nd Stage 0 DCIS breast cancer & polycythemia vera. Did a DBM with reconstruction, no chemo needed.

This time there wasn't as much fear with the diagnosis. You see, I have found strength in my cancer journey. I have found the strength and the courage to keep moving forward with my life's journey. There may be a stumble from time to time, but moving forward is all that matters.

Patti Carey - @pfastycarey

HELEN SMEDLEY

@helenstar50

I was diagnosed at 50 on 15.05.15 with Grade 3 Invasive Breast Cancer ER+ and PR+

It will be a shock when people who you considered close to you find it hard to be there for you, and you will be surprised where you find support and compassion. Some people cannot deal with or be around trauma, please remember this is no reflection on you, my advice is to surround yourself with loving like minded people, be kind to yourself, try not to be consumed by your thoughts and fears.

Moving forward is not easy and daily struggles continue for many years.

Please enjoy life, make those special memories, above all live each day without regret, seize the day and don't forget to breathe

I wrote this poem whilst taking part in a Moving Forward course at Maggie's back in 2020. I hope you find peace, love Helen 8 year survivor

PHILIP ALDERSON

A Quiet Mind

Constant voices, questions,

No answers,

Doubt, Fear, Loneliness,

Hot, Panic, Distress,

It is all in my head you said,

My head, my thoughts,

They are my thoughts, just my thoughts,

These voices are my thoughts,

My voice inside my head,

Slow down, Stop,

Step back, Notice,

Recognise, Let go, Engage,

Rise and fall,

Breathe,

Peace,

A Quiet Mind.

By Helen Smedley

Helen Smedley - @helenstar50

NATALIE MIZUIK

@nataliemariecoaching

I lost my beloved Mum to breast cancer in 2016 at the age of 72. It was the third time she had faced this gruelling diagnosis. Despite witnessing her struggle, I never imagined it could happen to me. I neglected regular breast checks, living as if I were invincible.

February 2023 shattered that illusion. While coaxing my three sons to get ready for school, a familiar routine, I detected a solid lump in my left breast. Having witnessed my husband's battle with melanoma of the ear the previous year, I was now programmed to act fast and rule out anything sinister. I promptly called the GP, securing an appointment and a mammogram referral that day.

I dismissed the lump as a blocked milk duct since I had recently weaned my then 12-month-old. Almost three weeks later, I underwent a mammogram which came back clear – no lumps detected. I was surprised and asked the technician how that could be, given I could clearly feel a lump under the skin. Apparently, breast density plays a big part in the accuracy of mammograms, especially in those who are younger. This was the first incident in which I learned the importance of advocating for your own health. The technician then took me down the hall for an ultrasound.

The ultrasound technician confirmed the lump and attributed it, most likely, to fibroadenoma. However, my family history of breast cancer prompted a biopsy just to be sure. A week later, I was told I had breast cancer. It was a shock, and even harder was not having any answers. When cancer is confirmed, the biopsy is sent away for pathology, and until then, we don't know the type, grade, or treatment plan.

A week later, following an agonizing wait, the chemotherapy flyers on the doctor's desk revealed the harsh reality – triple-negative breast cancer, grade 3.

Weeks of CT scans and MRIs told us it hadn't spread – a glimmer of positivity amongst the constant hammering of fear and unknowns. Since then, I've endured 16 rounds of 4 different types of chemotherapy, 17 rounds of immunotherapy, surgery, radiotherapy, and I'm about to start taking Capecitabine, an oral chemo, as post-surgery pathology disappointingly revealed residual cancer.

"You're so strong," "You're Superwoman," "You're an inspiration" – these are the constant affirmations I receive, along with the new one for 2023 – "You've got a great shaped head!" Yet, to me it just feels like I don't have a choice, much the same as any other cancer patient.

At times, I feel detached from my former self, but then I remember that I'm an evolved version, more resilient but also transformed by the unwavering support and love I've received and determined to pass on the kindness in every way possible. Facing mortality has taught me that life is a gift and it's meant to be lived. I'm determined to set healthy boundaries and embrace gratitude daily.

My advice to anyone facing a cancer diagnosis? Visualize a cherished moment in the distant future, picturing it vividly, every single day. Crystallize the details in your mind and believe it will happen. My vision is my now 1-year-old's 21st birthday party, where I stand before a crowd, supported by my three grown sons. It's a visual that brings me to tears every time because it's a statement of love, gratitude, and above all, hope.

Natalie Mizuik - @nataliemariecoaching

PHILIP ALDERSON

KELLY

@beyond_the_boob

Survival Tip For #Philaldobook @Philaldo

There are so many things to say about the cancer journey, so many different pieces of advice. There is no right or wrong way to handle it. We are all unique, in our diagnosis, in our treatment plans and in our physical and emotional selves.

I offer this advice on my approach to receiving chemo;

It's happening. Whether you want it to or not. You can either use your energy to resent it, or you can embrace it. I chose to embrace it. I pretended that each infusion, each time I was in the chair, I was on an airplane. Cut off from the real world for a few hours. I read, I napped, I chatted to the wonderful nurses (air stewardesses), I accepted the drinks and snacks. I would take a walk to the bathroom and stretch my legs. I used the time as best I could rather than begrudge being there. Eventually, after 16 rounds, I reached my destination.

My mentor and inspiration throughout my journey, the wonderful @thecharlottewroe

Kelly - @beyond_the_boob

SUSIE

@my_6pack_is_there_somewhere

"I'm Sorry, You Have Breast Cancer" 6 Little Words No One Ever Wants To Hear - Especially Not At 26!!

There was no family history!! So why me? Why anyone I guess!

One thing I've learnt since my diagnosis is that cancer does not discriminate. There is no point sitting in self pity because that doesn't change the outcome, however it has made me grab life and live it to the full.

I've raised over £150,000 for my local breast unit - something I wouldn't have done had I not have been diagnosed. I walked down a catwalk in London for Breast Cancer Now in front of 1500 people. I stripped naked for a charity calendar. Life does not have to stop - I'm 19 years on since hearing those awful words and I'm most certainly living my best life. Don't let cancer define you.

Susie - @my_6pack_is_there_somewhere

PHILIP ALDERSON

KATH HAMILTON

@katy_ham_lton

This Is My Second Time Around With Breast Cancer In 10 Years.

One song that has really helped keep me focused and upbeat is Jordin Sparks - one step at a time ....

Kath Hamilton - @katy_ham_lton

PHILIP ALDERSON

KATHY PAULSON

@Madkat68

I was diagnosed with oestrogen & progesterone positive breast cancer at 49. The cancer I had was aggressive & could not be seen on a mammogram. It lit up brilliantly on a ultrasound though. Please don't trust that a negative mammogram means there is nothing there. If you feel like there is something sinister, fight to have it rechecked.

What no one tells you is no amount of reconstruction, no matter how good, is going to return you to how you were before your surgeries & treatment. Reconstruction left me in & out of recovery for two years, and I was blessed with no complications. However, I was unable to do the things I love to do in life for much longer than if I'd gone flat. I couldn't ride my horse, practice archery, sew, or hike. I missed out on living life during that time. I think often we are in such a rush to prove to ourselves & others that this disease will not take over our life that we don't realize from the moment of diagnosis it actually does change you completely...

That's not necessarily a bad thing. It allows us to wake

up out ruts we've formed, sometimes existing instead of living.

Lastly, don't be afraid of tomorrow. My life and how I live is very different than it was. And it is good! This road definitely makes you look at what nonsense you might be putting up with that is just a waste of time & emotion. It's okay to move onto what YOU really want to invest yourself in.

CHEMO tips:

1. After round two, when your taste buds start to go and stay gone, choose foods to eat that you didn't normally eat. You won't know that they don't taste right because you're not used to eating them. It makes the food you do get to eat much more enjoyable if that's possible.

2. Season foods with vinegar based items, things like ketchup, mustard & flavored balsamic vinegars. One particularly wonderful memory I have is having a loaf of French bread and vanilla ice cream which I could not taste but used solely as delivery methods for blueberry, chocolate, maple and strawberry vinegars.

3. Lots of salads dressed in olive oil & flavored balsamic vinegars.

Kathy Paulson - @Madkat68

JO HAYES

@thedroppedlollipop

Audio: Always Look on the Bright Side of Life - Monty Python

Look For The Positives

In my forties I was made bankrupt and lost everything - my husband, my home, savings, friends, job, everything except my daughters.

It took a long time, but by the time I turned 50, I was settled in my own house, I had a good job and travelled more than ever, I found my true friends, was happy with my partner, and of course, I had my daughters. I did a charity parachute jump for my local hospice and was enjoying life again!

A month later I was told I had two types of breast cancer One in each breast. A 7cm lump and a 1cm lump were found by my first routine mammogram. I couldn't feel either of them and I had no symptoms.

I'd already been floored by so many things, and this was

another bump on the rocky road of life.

I had no choice but to get on with treatment and surgery, and all the side effects that came with it, and they weren't good. But looking for the bright side in everything is what has always got me through, staying positive, the love of family and friends and not wallowing in self pity. You CAN get through anything if you put your mind to it. However many times you get knocked down, just keep getting up, take one step at a time.

I've just turned 51, and my treatment has been successful, I have some wonderful new friends that I wouldn't have met without cancer, and I am so very grateful to still be here to live another day x

Lots of love,

Jo

Jo Hayes - @thedroppedlollipop

LAURA ASHURST

@lauraashurst_lwh

The Breath of Hope

The single cell that broke away

Cannot break my spirit.

The surgeon's knife that cut away

Cannot pierce my soul.

The heat from days of radiation

Cannot burn my heart.

The Hope that gently sits within it

Will not and cannot be harmed.

As I gently breathe and feel its flow,

In this present moment, I am alive.

Laura Ashurst - @lauraashurst_lwh

PHILIP ALDERSON

GEMMA HAYDOCK

@gemmahaydock

Audio: Sia - Unstoppable

Buckle Up Baby!

This is going to be a bumpy and scary ride and your strength and patience will be truly tested over the following years, but you can weather this storm, as you are far stronger than you ever imagined so use this strength and be proud of yourself!

Allow yourself to feel the fear this brings, but don't let it define you!

Control what you can, advocate for yourself!

Keep pushing forward with the biggest smile on your face, shining a light at the darkest of moments in your world.

Lean a little more on people who love you and let them surround you with support, as this journey is something you go onto together and not one to travel alone!

Right now there may seem like there is no end in sight, but I promise you, that the day will come where rainbows will form, the sun will shine so bright and you will be able to breathe again and you will look back at where you started, with so much pride and say 'I did it', 'I tackled something that seemed impossible

Gemma Haydock - @gemmahaydock

NIKKI SCOTT

@mrsnikkianne

The day before I was told that my lump in my breast was concerning, we buried my brother-in-law who has died from a brain tumour.

Even with cancer very much present in my family life, I still believed it was something that wouldn't happen to me and definitely not happen at such a young age. To me, breast cancer was something that affected ladies who were older.

Once the reality began to sink in, the questions then began to take over my brain ... why me? did I do something to cause it? But what I learned is that it didn't matter. The facts were simple and I had to just take it, head on and fight! And that's what I would say to everyone embarking on this journey - fight!

This process is hard. There are good and bad days but there are also amazing days - you just have to allow yourself to have them. Cancer will now be a part of you, but it doesn't have to define you or completely take over either. Make the most of the days you feel good and well

- go out for that walk, meet that friend, go sledging or whatever activity you know you'll enjoy. But it's also so important to know that it's okay to have days where you cry, or you're angry. Let all of those emotions out - it really does help!

Your outlook on life will change and that's okay. Embrace the changes. You'll have new appreciation for all aspects of life, you'll find silver linings in places you may never have before and you'll love those around you even more deeply for the help and support they give you during this time.

Keep smiling.

Keep fighting.

Keep surviving.

Nikki

Nikki Scott - @mrsnikkianne

KATIE

@notoriouskga

A Year On From Breast Cancer Diagnosis

As I rapidly approach my one year anniversary since diagnosis I'm in a reflective mood.

It's got me thinking. What would I say to someone who was recently diagnosed or about to start treatment?

First and foremost we're all very different, our treatments are individual as are our experiences.

I was terrified starting treatment comparing myself to others 'journeys' and although I gained solace in connecting with many a different person, I also found it hard seeing what was potentially to come.

For me it was and is important to take things at my own pace and never to feel pressured. I'm a control freak and when I was diagnosed everything spiralled and everything was very much out of my comfort zone.

Small things have allowed me to feel less chaotic such as wearing the @scalpcooling, it slowed down the process of hair loss and allowed me to control when/if I wanted to shave my head.

Picking and choosing how I wanted to get to the hospital and who I wanted there and how I wanted to do things moving forward.

For example my chemo ward was initially small and visitors were asked not to join unless under certain circumstances so I always chose to be alone (although you're never truthfully alone with the amazing nurses and other patients).

For me dealing with emotions has always been a solitary experience, perhaps unhealthy but if I'm nervous, I prefer to do things alone. Having treatment is hardcore for everyone, not just the patient so seeing/hearing others concerns and fears can be too much.

Looking back over the last year I've definitely found peace with sharing my experience and emotions, it's unraveled a lot not just the cancer itself but many other aspects of my life. It's been actually cathartic.

However:

'If you don't schedule a break, your body will take one for you'

Ain't that the truth!!!

K A T I E - @notoriouskga

FIONA

@microbladingandmorefiona

Aged 32 I started to gain weight, get hot flushes and feel terribly emotional. Then I found a lump in my breast.

I visited the GP after having bloods taken and she advised I was going through an early menopause and sent me off to see fertility specialists as I was yet to start a family.

A couple of weeks later she telephoned me and apologised she had misread my blood results. I wasn't going through menopause, but more than likely had breast cancer!

Within a week I was having my first chemo after being diagnosed with triple positive, stage 3 breast cancer and DCIS. It was also in my lymph nodes.

Looking back I realised there were also differences in my breast, in that the bottom of it had flattened and the nipple had puckered. But despite all of these things, I didn't approach my GP until I found a lump.

I think the most important thing is to know your normal and seek help if anything at all changes. I thought I was too young for breast cancer, or anything serious to be honest so that would be something I would raise with my younger self if I could.

However, I don't think I would change the fact I've had breast cancer. I've always been a caring and considerate person, but this illness and the immense difficulties it throws upon you and the fear, totally changes your perspective on life.

I'm not sure I would enjoy things as much as I do now without having had it. I ask my areola tattoo ladies the same thing and they often say they wouldn't change having joined this club.

For me, it meant difficulties in having a child, but after 7 IVF attempts I got lucky! I had waited a long time to have my baby so didn't want to go back to financial services and the long hours and travel this involved, so I left my 26 year career and retrained as a medical and cosmetic tattooist.

I now spend my days giving brows to those heading into chemo, or tattooing areolas for those post mastectomy and completing their journey. I love love love what I do and couldn't be more passionate about it.

Training other artists to complete these heroes is another level and they come from around the globe to learn.

I consider having had breast cancer a privilege which has opened up so many doors for me to be able to help others with empathy, compassion and an unspoken understanding that I know where they're coming from.

Breast cancer has changed my life in many ways, I may have wonky boobs and crazy curly hair that I can't deal with, but I enjoy and appreciate everything on a different level and have the most rewarding job in the world! X

Fiona - @microbladingandmorefiona

JESSICA AIDEM

@fightlikeagirl_fit

*Audio: Bebe Rexha -
On every run*

Through My Eyes

I was diagnosed at 35 years old. A mommy to four children ages 6, 4, 3, and 2 and my life shattered when I heard the words, "Breast Cancer, Her 2+."

First things first I was under the knife removing EVERYTHING because I was not messing around with their offer of a lumpectomy with chemo & radiation to follow. I said "no I will be doing a double mastectomy including nipple & areola removal with Chemo & no radiation"

Once I lost a part of my body that played such a huge role in my life feeding my four babies, I went into hiding. I realized no one could help me or save me and I had to "Trust The Process" of Chemotherapy that was stripping me raw. I knew I could only help myself at this point as I was going through a divorce, a mom of four little ones battling for my life, and my heart was breaking

I flourished the minute I turned to myself and gave my breaking self no other option but up and moving. This looked like stretching on days that were bad, getting on my spin bike on better days, pushing even harder on great days completing workouts from home, and eventually began my running journey

Showing up for myself as much as I could daily created a pattern, which created a feeling and that feeling has now become a habit

This led me to happiness and forgiveness, a place of feeling stronger mentally and physically, and simply just knowing that I was building my body back to life through movement was powerful

Movement created circulation to ease the body aches, while Juicing replenished my body with each stripping round of Chemotherapy

"When Life gets tough, plant your feet & hold on tight, ride the waves until YOU come back." - Jessica Aidem

#breastcancer #survivor #giving #givingback #givingbacktothecommunity #someonessurvivalguide #philaldobook #noonefightsalone #smallprint #itsme #fightlikeagirlfit

Jessica Aidem - @fightlikeagirl_fit

JO HAMMOND

@jo.hammond.5

My first 'encounter' with breast cancer was when i was about 15 and my auntie Shirley died from the disease. Growing up i always remember my mum and her sisters finding lumps in their boobs that were always harmless cysts. Fast forward to 2012 and my mum found a lump which she instantly knew was different to all the others. She was diagnosed with triple negative breast cancer just before Christmas that year. Straight away she opted for a mastectomy and fortunately the cancer hadn't spread and after a round of chemotherapy she was given the all clear.

The family history meant me and my older sister would need mammograms from the age of 40. Stupidly i never checked my boobs, i think i was too scared of finding something. Right in the middle of the pandemic in June 2020 i was laying in bed one night when i had an itch on my boob. As i scratched it i thought i felt a lump. After another feel i realised there was definitely something there. After the weekend i made a dr's appointment, something told me not to leave it. I saw the nurse who assured me she knew her breast lumps and was certain it was just a cyst but she would refer me just incase due to my family history.

As i was walking home i received a text for an appointment at the breast clinic the following week. I knew i would be having a biopsy, an ultrasound and a mammogram but i didn't know i'd be getting the results the same day so i went in by myself.

After all the tests i waited for hours, everyone else was getting called back in and leaving and i was still sat there. Eventually i was called back in and told whilst my mammogram was clear the ultrasound had shown something and i would need an MRI. I literally fell apart.

A week later i was back at the hospital as my biospy results had come in. I never expected to hear those words of "you have cancer" so again i went in by myself. I should have known as soon as i walked in the room to be greeted by the breast surgeon and a breast cancer nurse that it was going to be bad news.

I had stage 1, grade 1 breast cancer. Thankfully it had been caught early and as long as everything stayed as it was my treatment plan was relatively straightforward, a lumpectomy, radiotherapy and tamoxifen. I would need to be genetically tested and we were still waiting for the her2 results so there were a lot of what if's at that stage.

The single best piece of advice my surgeon gave me that day was "focus on what we know now" and honestly that was invaluable to me and is something i always say to people i meet who are newly diagnosed.

A cancer diagnosis is a minefield of information and your mind can definitely go in to overdrive. Following her advice definitely helped me through those early days. Thankfully my genetics test was negative and so was the her2 test. The cancer hadnt spread and my operation was successful in removing it all. The only thing was the MRI had detected a second, smaller lump which was also cancerous. This meant i was going to loose a fair chunk of my boob so i opted for a li-cap procedure where they reconstruct the breast using back fat. They were able to do this at the same time as my lumpectomy so i only had to have 1 surgery. About six weeks after my operation i had radiotherapy over 9 days and then started on Tamoxifen.

I found life after treatment the hardest to navigate. I had been on auto pilot for 3 months, hospital appointment after hospital appointment and just focusing on getting through each stage and suddenly after treatment that all stopped and i felt very alone.

Having cancer taught me a few things. I am stronger than i ever thought i would be, I am more resiliant than i ever dreamed i could be and you have to live you life, make every second count because it could all be taken away from you in a moment.

I am now 3 years clear and i am using my experience to help others. I constantly spread awareness and encourage others to check themselves and see their GP if they find anything that doesnt feel normal to them. Ive also done a lot of fundraising for Breast Cancer Now and Future Dreams House and challenged myself to do things i never thought possible. I always thought cancer was a death sentence but my mum showed me it doesnt have to be that way, her strength gave me strength to fight and we both showed cancer who's boss.

PHILIP ALDERSON

Jo Hammond - @jo.hammond.5

SAM PARR

@samparrart

Audio: Gotta get thru this / Daniel Bedingfield

You'll Have Great Days, Some Bad Days, But Not Every Day And You Can Still Do Lots Of Stuff

Inspired and guided by the awesome @oriordanliz who has been and continues to be a voice of gentle comfort, empowering knowledge, expertise and a dedication to all things breast cancer and breast cancer patients and survivors. But what to say, where to start?

About surviving breast cancer. Know this, it will change you. Forever. Beyond treatment, beyond "recovery" - in a way you never recover. Your life, your body, your mind, your heart, will be forever marked. You will grieve the you that is lost forever.

But, you will learn, you will grow, in so many ways. You'll find strength you never knew you had. And it will pull into laser focus the importance of every moment, every hour, every day, every year. The preciousness of it. The privilege of it. And that is a wonderful gift. Pity those that do not understand. You understand. And that is a beautiful thing. Life will go on, you will go on. Everything ends. So live now. As you wish to. Only you know what you want.

Give yourself the nearest version of your perfect life that you can. You deserve it.

Sam Parr - @samparrart

CARLY MOOSAH

@carlymoosah

Please Don't Say It's Just Hair. It Will Grow Back. Try Not To Care.

It's not just hair it's so much more. It's heartache. It's pain with each strand on the floor.

It's shedding an identity of all that I knew. It's deep vulnerability through and through.

It's no longer being able to hide the cancer within. It screams I'm a patient with each new bald patch of skin.

It's hard to look at mirrors & not recognise who I see. Transforming & no longer feeling like me.

And as the hair starts to come back with a life of its own. It represents hope with each inch that is grown.

Please don't say it's just hair. It does grow back. I massively care.

Carly Moosah - @carlymoosah

PHILIP ALDERSON

MIA DAVIES

@miadaviesphotography

My Story

When I was diagnosed I was desperately trying to find answers or read people's stories online. Anywhere I could find written words on how I was expected to get through the next however long (I say however long because I definitely still have days of wondering how to navigate it). The day I heard the words 'we're pretty sure what we've found is cancer' (ergh, still sends shivers through my body) I messaged a lady I knew who had been through the same thing and within an hour was on her doorstep.

I'd probably start my advice with the complete opposite thing to what I did and don't rely on other people's advice as a whole, read the stories and take bits you believe will help you but there is so much of finding your feet as you go and before you know it, you're the one with tips and advice for others.

With chemo I read SO much that my mind was overwhelmed with tips and tricks that I thought would help me through and although some things did, there was so much that I could not physically (or mentally I guess) do as my body didn't have the energy to. People at the start told me to avoid certain foods (sugar, meat etc etc) - that absolutely did not happen. I was hardly able to eat and when I did I continuously threw up so it is defo a case of eat what you can, when you can. Even if that's a McDonalds milkshake at 11pm, go with the cravings whenever you get them as trying to get food (and especially fluid) into you is so important, so take it when you can.

Accept the help, accept defeat some days and accept the fact that you have to take time out for you and not worry about replying to texts/emails etc, or if you want to do that, do it.

I'm basically saying, do whatever YOU need to do to help YOU.

Forget about anyone else around you and focus fully on YOU!

Good friends will still reach out and not expect anything back, they'll know you'll come to them when you are ready. If you have kids like I do, let them have fun days out with family or friends, try to let them live a normal life as possible.

That helps you mentally. Just focus on YOU.

Mia Davies - @miadaviesphotography

JODI HOLLAND

@the_skin_trainer

The Power Of Positive Self Talk

Myself and my legend of a Dad both fought and beat #Cancer at the same time.

If there's one thing he taught me during our journey, that I would pass on to others it was The Power Of Positive Self Talk.

My dad simply refused to let his #Leukaemia beat him, and I honestly believe that mindset went a long way in aiding his recovery, and subsequently mine too!

Positive Self Talk is a powerful tool for shaping your mindset. When you consciously use positive and affirming language in your thoughts and inner dialogue, it has several benefits...

1 By reinforcing positive messages to yourself, you can counteract negative thoughts, self-doubt, and fears

2 It helps build self-confidence and can contribute to improved emotional wellness

3 It leads to increased motivation, resilience, and a more

constructive approach to challenges (the medical team at Bristol Oncology nicknamed my dad the Lion)

4 Positive self-talk can also impact your interactions with others, as a confident and optimistic mindset often radiates through your words and actions

The power of positive self talk lies in it's ability to shape your perception of yourself and the world around you

We sadly lost my dad to Encephalitis in November 2019, but his positive fighting spirit will forever live on.

#mysurvivaladvice #philaldobook #someonessurvivalguide @philaldo book

Jodi Holland - @the_skin_trainer

EMMA YOUNG

@theweecandme

Emma, Diagnosed With Stage 1, Grade 3 Tnbc June 2022, The Same Day That A Family Friend Passed Away With The Same Disease.

I had 16 weeks of chemo, an operation then radiotherapy. Treatment finished in December 2022.

I could hear my breast cancer nurse saying, "this is a curative disease!" And curative is what I was going for. My determined Emma mode kicked in. As a single parent to two little girls my battle wasn't just about me.

Through chemo I had a square of raw jelly everyday to help my nails. I kept them and the jelly was quite nice.

Motivational blogs, @philaldo giving me a daily giggle with the memes has to be @theboobbattle. I was following her well before I even discovered a lump.

I've connected with so many people through instagram. I never wanted my wee page to be a sympathy seeker but more an opportunity to raise awareness and prod people to check their boobs.

DAWN JEHLE

@wonkywarriors

Breast Cancer Is Not Pink And Fluffy. And Post Cancer Recovery Is Nothing To Be Sniffed At Either.

I wish I had taken my recovery more seriously. I buried my head in the sand for so long and did not give it the attention and respect it was due.

If you are past your active treatment and starting to pick up the pieces of your life, please take a breath. Acknowledge what you have been through. It's the first step forward...

Butterflies and Blisters... A poem...

It's a long walk, this road to recovery.

Certain it would lead me back home,

I started out with the best of intentions,

And that it was a journey I could make on my own.

But it's a long walk, this road to recovery.

The path is not straight from pain to healing.

Certain my defenses would protect my soul

I started out with my shield and my sword,

Thinking all it would take was a little control.

But the path is not straight from pain to healing.

It feels more like a mountain or being lost at sea

When the darkness descends and there's nowhere to flee

You can't catch your breath and fall to your knees

Under the weight of your grief, you just want to be free…

It's in those dark lonely moments when you honour your pain,

Put down your burdens and lift your face to the rain.

When you finally acknowledge your scars and your fears,

That's when recovery begins, with those first healing tears.

This is just the start of the journey.

So put down your sword, it's no longer a fight.

The ground beneath your feet is a well-trodden path.

Take a deep breath and fill your soul with the light.

This is just the start of the journey.

It's a long walk, this road to recovery.

But I found joy on this path of butterflies and blisters

Once I finally figured out that there's no going back.

And I'm so glad I found you, my brothers and sisters.

Because whilst it's a long walk, this road to recovery…

… We do not have to travel it alone.

~ Dawn Jehle ~

Dawn Jehle - @wonkywarriors

PHILIP ALDERSON

GAYE NOBLE-WOOTTON

@maddysmum1

April 2014 I found a lump, visit to my doctor who thought it was a cyst. He sent me on an urgent referral and 2 weeks later I visited the hospital. The consultant there again though it was a cyst but would send me to get an ultrasound and mammogram. The consultant there was concerned about a patch she could see on there but wasn't being picked up on the mammogram. A biopsy was taken from both areas and results would be a week later. Hubby asked if he wanted him to go with me, I said I'd be fine. A week later when 3 people entered the room my heart sank and my brain went FUCK. I knew then that it was cancer. The consultant gave me a hug and said I'm so sorry and my breast nurse Michelle handed me tissues while I phoned my hubby.

That night he didn't want to go to work but I told him I needed him to go so I could get my head around it. I shouted, screamed and cried until something clicked and from somewhere a sense of calm came over me. Right you bastard, I though, you're not having me. I've too much to live for. My boy was turning 3 in a few weeks.

Sentinel node biopsy was booked in for 21st May. No one warned me when I came around that I would have wee that looked like I'd swallowed a bluloo!! I had to ask if this was normal...

I was found to have pre-cancerous cells in my sentinel node and meant a full lymph node clearance. They wanted me to go in on 3rd June, my son's 3rd birthday. It was rearranged for 10th. I had also opted for a double mastectomy but my consultant persuaded me to have them done separately, also to have surgery before any other treatment. Having a good surgeon and a good relationship with them did make the whole process much easier. Surgery came and I woke up with drains, bandages and an immediate reconstruction. After a few days in hospital due to low oxygen levels, I went home. Getting used to the drains and not leaving them hanging on the radiator when having a wash was a lesson itself. After a long 3 weeks they were all out and a week later I was back to work. Chemo followed at the end of July, I managed the whole 6 sessions.

It wasn't easy, my main symptoms being fatigue and a taste like gone off cream cakes, losing my hair and eyebrows. December brought radiotherapy, 25 sessions which finished at the beginning of January 2015. After a few months tamoxifen arrived, luckily didn't have too many side effects from this, mainly hand cramps. In March I became a volunteer for the then Breast Cancer Care on their someone like me team. December, after much arguing with the hospital, my second mastectomy was completed. At this time reconstruction patients weren't considered a priority, but eventually was carried out. The following January I had both implants expanded. For 3 months everything was great. Then I noticed my right side was getting smaller and going north. Not a great look.

Trying to get this sorted was the beginning of a 3 year nightmare which eventually resulted in a formal apology from my hospital and a change in procedure regarding treatment of reconstruction patients. They are now treated with the same respect as newly diagnosed cancer patients. And finally in 2019 my implant was changed, and fingers crossed, everything is still OK.

Gaye Noble-Wootton - @maddysmum1

PHILIP ALDERSON

DIANE CASTRO

@layayi

Cancer Will Not Take My Joy!

During "Pink October" in 2011, I had a routine mammogram. Then an ultrasound. Then a biopsy. Turned out I had metastatic invasive ductal carcinoma, stage 3b, and had to have multiple surgeries and 18 weeks of chemo.

I had already had my first round of chemo and my hair had started to fall out. My grandson Johan was 3 years old and I was worried that he would not recognize me, or worse - would be afraid when he saw me. So we had decided, in advance, to fly out to see him and let him help shave my head.

My son Jason shaved my husband's head first, Johan was cool with it. Then I told him I was going to shave my head...he didn't believe me! He actually laughed and said "Wela, you're crazy!" We explained that I was sick and had to take some strong medicine and I showed him my port and let him touch it. He said I was a superhero...just like Tony Stark aka Iron Man! I was Iron Wela. It was a fun day.

I am sharing this to let you know that cancer did

not take my joy, it made me fight to live in order to enjoy more moments and make more memories with my grandson...and the rest of my family

If you have any health concern, please make sure you get checked ASAP! Early detection/diagnosis and treatment is key.

#breastcancerawareness #breastcancer #ifightlikeagirl #savethetatas #pinkoctober

Diane Castro - @layayi

BISBROOKE ARTISANS

@ami_bisbrooke_artisans

It's Not Just Hair

Even though I embraced my bald head look and appreciated the edgy image, I remember my long blonde hair and the fear I felt as clumps of it fell out in the shower in my hands! Then as I looked in the mirror and saw bald patches I felt anxious and distressed. Suddenly the sobering reality of my cancer and losing my identity hit hard.

But acceptance of loss is a quiet inner affair. It's a dark lonely place where to be as brave as people think you are, you have to dig deep, face your fears and trust that you're more amazing than you know and stronger than you can imagine.

And you find out that tears, sorrow and pain are your companions to healing.

So a few tears later, I chose to shave it all off in one go and asked Georgia - my daughter- to use the clippers. And I couldn't stop making some jokes throughout.

That was me putting on a brave face. I really couldn't do it any other way.

Then as we filmed it I realised that being brave is exactly that - still afraid but then going ahead.

Then fleetingly, there's an excitement of the new as I looked in the mirror. A smooth bald head! Soon I was exploring different clothes, make up so for awhile being bald felt dynamic and I learnt to love this new face. My expressions seemed open and it was more about my energy rather than my hair.

This has been quite a revelation. And as I look back with self compassion for myself, I can literally hug this Ami. Even though some people said 'oh it's only hair and it'll grow back' I know it was never just hair. It's a massive identity loss. And it's not vanity. It's a raw experience where you are literally stripped of your crowning glory. It's different if you choose to have a buzz cut because that's a hair style choice. I didn't choose.

My hair did of course grew back just as we knew it would. I danced throughout my hair loss and re- growth because while it didn't take away my loss it did help me to connect with and find my joy.

Grief isn't asking for pity. But space to do it's work. And it's in this space that I find myself and love who I am.

How do you feel about your hair?

Bisbrooke Artisans - @ami_bisbrooke_artisans

ALIKI DAR

@ibc_journey_of_aliki

What I Thought Was Going To Be My Survival Guide Vs. How I Actually Survived

"The worst part of cancer is the treatment."

For me, the worst part was the period between the diagnosis and the beginning of treatment. Endless scans, tests, talks, waiting and getting even more stressed. Once that was done and some of my sanity was left, it felt as if I was halfway there.

"Starting treatment will be scary."

For me, starting treatment felt empowering in a way. Terrifying, yes, but I was finally doing something and was fighting.

"Losing your hair and losing your identity"

Hair loss because of chemo wasn't that bad in my case. Slowly turning into a minion (colour, shape, and all) was what broke my vanity. But I learnt to appreciate my looks, and I got ready to welcome the new me, scars, and all.

"You will be too sick to eat."

I wasn't. I could smell everything and was salivating. But my taste buds were one of the first things to go with chemo, and everything tasted rotten or like butter... Even water felt like drinking oil. I was starving. And always disappointed when I ate. But I kept eating to nourish my body for the fight. And I made a list of all the foods I was going to eat once the chemo was done. I'm still going through that list. Repeatedly.

"Scanxiety is scary."

Scanxiety is paralysing. Period.

"You will get sick with no immune system due to chemo treatment."

Yes. But nothing can prepare you for how physically weak you will be, how crippling that can feel, and the discouragement along with it. This is where you rely heavily (both physically and emotionally) on your people.

"Depression and resentment"

As I got sicker from the chemo, the feeling of all this being so unfair kept creeping up. I lashed out at loved ones, who forgave me, but I still feel terrible at doing so. Sharing my journey on social media stopped me from turning in a purple minion (without the hair).

"Sarcasm and dark humour"

If I thought I couldn't become more sarcastic, I was so wrong! I made jokes left right and centre and dared to make the "bad" ones, because, well... I could and still can get away with them. Discovering this part of myself was a joy.

"Losing yourself"

Yes. The old me is lost. I miss her, and I wish I had appreciated her more. But the new me is here, and I'm getting to know her, and I see her being fearless, funny, relaxed, but not taking things for granted and more appreciative. And I find it interesting how cancer made me not give a crap and my best self was revealed.

There's more, and I could go on and on. Everyone's cancer journey and experience is different. But it does help to share it and feel less alone.

#philaldobook

Thank you @philaldo for this wonderful idea!!!❤

Aliki Dar - @ibc_journey_of_aliki

PHILIP ALDERSON

KELSIE DAVIES

@kels_1972

Audio: King King - What ever it takes to survive

My Breast Cancer Survival Guide!

Tbh I wasn't going to participate in the @philaldo book when asked... I was at an all time low having just gone through chemo cycle 3 & was really struggling mentally, physically & emotionally. But with cycle 4 looming & having to give myself a talking to so I can do it again, I thought perhaps I do have some advice....

• This time is only temporary & it will pass, it will feel like it goes on forever but it doesn't. You are stronger & more resilient than you ever thought possible.

• Like many times in your life you will lose friends, this is not your fault... either they weren't the friends you thought they were or they are finding it hard for some reason. Try to give friends that you feel have abandoned you the benefit of the doubt, perhaps they love you more than you thought & are struggling with you being ill.

Let your true friends if they want to feel useful, let them

be. Let them mop the tears, cry with you, cook for you, run errands, or attend hospital appointments to keep you company. You will find you are loved more than you realise. Virtual strangers will reach out. Renewing your faith in human kindness.

• Get outside even when you feel like it's impossible, exercise, nature & fresh air will help you both physically & mentally.

• Most of all be kind to you, don't say anything to yourself you wouldn't say to your best friend if they were in the same boat. You've got this, its perfectly OK to withdraw, cry & be angry... this will pass. You are only human.

• Find a BC buddy... someone who knows how you feel... I met @misslaurenwebb online & she's kept me going at times, checking in on me & me her. Someone to share & understand your journey.

• I'm passionate about music & the track " What ever it takes to survive " by my favourite band @kingkinguk has taken on a very different meaning to me. I draw strength from the track.

Most inspirational person for me has been @oriordanliz her book & advice has been a life saver! As a breast cancer patient & breast cancer surgeon she has the knowledge & compassion that i needed ❤

Kelsie Davies - @kels_1972

SINEAD GRAVILL

@feeling_a_right_tit

When you hear the words "you've got cancer", prepare for your life to completely change. It becomes the "norm" when it really shouldn't. But take strength wherever you can.

Take each day at a time and try not to think too far ahead. Small, manageable chunks are what helped me. One day you'll hopefully be contributing to someone else's survival guide, even just by being there. Grab life and make the most of the good times. No, you will never be the same, but you will appreciate the little things so much more. @philaldo

I've been inspired by so many people through my cancer times, but at the moment I'm inspired by @jessicaszpigel ☆

PHILIP ALDERSON

DIANDRA

@cancer.free.haven

Audio: "Praise You In This Storm" by Casting Crowns

"Healing Is Coming To Wholeness"

Dear Cancer Survivor,

Your journey is uniquely yours, personal and powerful. In this guide, I hope you discover a source of comfort, a reminder that even in the toughest times, you're not alone.

Looking back at the early days after my new diagnosis, I reflected on the unexpected busyness that comes with it. Here's something I want you to remember: It's perfectly okay to set boundaries, to say no, and to shape your own schedule. This journey is yours; don't feel rushed or pressured into doing more than you're comfortable with.

I encourage you to take moments for yourself. Cancer can feel like a whirlwind, but it's crucial to center yourself. This isn't a battle; this is your health. You deserve those moments to breathe and gather strength.

As I started on my cancer journey for a second time, "The Book of Joy" by the Dalai Lama and Archbishop Desmond Tutu became my sanctuary. A specific chapter on "Illness and Fear of Death" really hit home. The wisdom of these men, finding joy amidst suffering, might just resonate with you as it did with me.

Whenever doubts cloud your mind, hold on to this quote from the book: "Healing is coming to wholeness and can happen whether or not the illness is curable." I repeated this quote to myself daily during those early days and it shifted my focus from seeking a cure to embracing healing in every sense.

Your body is incredible, just like mine. It's been through a lot, but it's not about fighting; it's about helping your body heal and move forward.

As you immerse yourself in this guide, remember it's your journey, and there's strength in every step you take. You've got this.

Sending you strength and healing vibes.

Diandra - @cancer.free.haven

ALEX PERRY

@her_bodywear

My cancer journey has been a bit of a sh*t show to be honest. With loads of challenges but also a few triumphs... I have the BRCA2 gene mutation and so does every single person in my family (male and female) from my granddad down. I knew that I wanted to undergo preventive surgery, but after having my first child, I also knew I wanted to breastfeed him first. So, at 29, when he was just three months old, I started trying to wean him off the boob so I could prepare for my surgery.

But things took an unexpected turn. They initially thought they had found DCIS (ductal carcinoma in situ) but in fact it turned out worse; the countless biopsies and scans revealed a mass that I would never have found. Therefore, it wasn't just going to be preventative surgery anymore. I was facing breast cancer surgery and treatments. But to add to the turmoil, I was in a toxic relationship that I struggled to leave. It felt like my world was so uncertain, on one hand I had the best thing I could ever wish for, the joy of having my baby but on the other hand the fear of facing the worst thing possible.

The surgeries and treatments that followed seem like

a distant faded memory now, but I remember feeling broken and paranoid. I was given a 5-year prescription for Tamoxifen… but then after just six months, I found out I was pregnant again… and I also found out that tamoxifen could potentially be very damaging to my unborn child, and I was advised to consider terminating the pregnancy. Knowing that tamoxifen was imperative to my recovery, i had to make a choice that I had no idea how to navigate. Me or my baby. I felt completely alone. Everyone thought I was crazy stopping the drug, but I knew I wanted my baby. I split up with my husband, and somehow found the courage to take this journey alone.

When my second son was born healthy in 2015, I felt like the luckiest person alive. I had battled disease, and then was rewarded with this miracle—I couldn't believe my luck.

In the hospital I actually found it quite funny when the nurse rather insensitively asked me why I didn't want to try to breast feed my baby. She said "do you want me to help you give it a go?".. I replied "well I think we would struggle. Last time I checked a double mastectomy with implants don't produce milk" lol.

Life slowly started to fall into place. I got my own house, my independence, and a fresh start. But then just as I finished my five years course of Tamoxifen, another breast cancer diagnosis struck, and it was right at the beginning of the covid lockdown in 2020. I had to face it all over again, alone.

I knew I was strong, I was optimistic, I felt like a warrior, but I also conflictingly felt like I was not emotionally equipped to deal with this burden. I was so scared, and the fear I felt waiting for the results of my scans was paralyzing. I remember having to face the thought of writing a will, wondering who will look after my boys for me, how I was going to make it.

But guess what I fucking made it. I got through it again. I might not be rich, but I have all the wealth I could wish for!! And I am HAPPY!

Alex Perry - @her_bodywear

PHILIP ALDERSON

JOELY A. SERINO

@beautifulmesspoetess

THEY SAY THAT I'M A
WARRIOR NOW.
A PART OF SOME
ELITE CLUB.
MY INITIATION THE STRANDS
THAT LAY ON MY BATHROOM FLOOR
BUT I'M NO HERO.
I'M NO WARRIOR.
THE ONLY BATTLE I'VE FOUGHT
IS THE ONE AGAINST THE COWARD
THAT IS CURRENTLY
SQUATTING THE AVAILABLE SPACE
IN MY HEAD.
I WILLINGLY LAY ON MY SWORD
AT LEAST TWO TIMES A DAY.

MY LIPS STUMBLE ACROSS THE
BEAUTIFUL WORDS THAT I
BEFRIENDED LONG AGO.
AND FAT TEARS FALL HEAVY
WITH MEMORIES LINING THE
PATH TO MY RECOVERY.
FILLING MY AIRWAYS.
DROWNING ME IN MY SLEEP,
A SUFFOCATION OF SCREAMS
JOLTING ME AWAKE.
TELL ME,
WHEN WILL THE NIGHTMARES STOP?
TELL ME THE NIGHTMARES WILL STOP.
- JOELY A. SERINO
@BEAUTIFULMESSPOETESS

Joely A. Serino - @beautifulmesspoetess

NATALIE WHIPPS

@natz.whipps

This poem was sent to me by some amazing friends when I was first diagnosed in June 2021. The friends are sisters and had been through a tough bereavement and had found comfort in this poem so they shared it with me.

It's by @lauradingedwards and I just love it. I hope this helps someone else who has been diagnosed with breast cancer and is as scared as I was.

#breastcancerawarenessadvocate #bcsurvivor

if the mountain seems too big today then climb a hill instead

if the morning brings you sadness it's ok to stay in bed

if the day ahead weighs heavy and your plans feel like a curse

there's no shame in rearranging, don't make yourself feel worse if a shower stings like needles and a bath feels like you'll drown

if you haven't washed your hair for days, don't throw away your crown

a day is not a lifetime, a rest is not defeat

don't think of it as failure just a quiet, kind retreat

it's ok to take a moment from an anxious fractured mind

the world will not stop turning while you get realigned

the mountain will still be there when you want to try again

you can climb it in your own time just love yourself til then

Laura Ding Edwards - (Reproduced with permission)

Natalie Whipps - @natz.whipps

SAM EVERETT

@_sam.everett_

Cancer Club

Cancer.

The club no-one ever wants to be a member of.

First rule of cancer club...No googling random cancer shit!

Yes,The internet can be a great source of information. But it is also a melting pot of mis-Information. Use it wisely. Use reputable sites such as Breast Cancer Now, or Macmillan for information you can trust.

Personally I found great comfort & support on social media.

Wait! Hear Me Out...

Inspired by " Ticking Off Breast Cancer " by Sarah Liyanage, I found a wealth of information, mainly on Instagram. At first it may seem intimidating, and very overwhelming but you will be welcomed. Look at your own pace, in your own time. Gradually you'll find people or posts will jump out at you, or resonate with you. These will become the building blocks of your very own support system. Although comparisons between what you see on social media & yourself are inevitable, please try to remember that every story is unique.

For me the toughest part, where I've needed most help is the emotional side of it all. Especially now the regular contact with medical staff has ended. I thought I was left to deal with the aftermath alone. But there, in my phone, is a support network of people who just "get it". A safe space where you don't have to try to explain or justify the way you're feeling.

At the time of writing, I've just passed 1 year of treatment ending and it's given me cause to reflect.

CANCER IS FUCKING SHIT!

It has left me physically less, battered, and scarred. Yet I have found I am more loved than I ever dreamt. I have gained a new perspective on life & things I want to focus on. Yet I live in contradictions, I want to push my limits while wanting to stay in my comfort zone and heal. I live with a body I no longer trust, while feeling damn proud of it.

Having a breast cancer diagnosis is fucking hard. You can't go through it alone.

Family and friends will want to help. Let them. They can provide practical help.

You will also need to TALK.

There are many in person resources, like Maggie's Centers. If you can't get out the house, Breast Cancer Now offer a phone service called Someone Like Me where you're matched with someone who has gone through similar experiences, with the same type of cancer as you.

But remember this is YOUR STORY, no one else's. DO CANCER YOUR WAY.

Although you may feel it, YOU ARE NOT ALONE,

We are here for you xx

#FuckCancer

Sam Everett - @_sam.everett_

PHILIP ALDERSON

HAYLEY GULLEN

@hayleygullen

Audio: Patrick Wolf - Accident and Emergency

Remember That Doctors And Nurses Are People Too

What got me through my treatment was finding human connection. The treatment itself is so dehumanising. You're reduced to a set of symptoms. A cog in a machine. I felt an overwhelming need to express myself and assert my individuality.

I had the idea to draw cartoon cards: firstly a new baby card for my surgeon, then a Christmas card (see my posts). These really did make a difference and went some way to bridging the divide between patient and doctor/nurse. Humour is a powerful tool.

And now I've nearly finished a graphic novel. I'd never have dreamed that was possible for me before.

So I'd say: if you have an opportunity to cross that divide, take it. Don't hold back out of shyness. Use your creativity to express your humanity.

And remember that the doctors and nurses are people too. If you want them to recognise your humanity, make sure you recognise theirs.

#philaldobook   #graphicmedicine   #breastcancer #breastcancerunder40   #breastcancerjourney #breastcancerawareness #breastcancersurvivors

Hayley Gullen - @hayleygullen

HANNAH LOUISE

@hannah_and_the_big_c

Being diagnosed with cancer is like someone handing you a fast track ticket to a destination unknown, your just bundled on to a train with no idea how many stops or how many destinations you will pass before your journey reaches your stop.

You don't know where that stop will be or for how long you will be allowed to stay there, some of us may stay a while and some may not.

Being diagnosed with cancer is like being entered into the world's shittest lottery, who knows what you'll get drawn.

Many times along this journey you may scream and cry and want to press the bell and get off at the next stop and that's normal, this is scary and unknown but I strongly believe we just have to ride the journey the best we can, with as much positivity as we can.

Sometimes the views will be incredible along the way and sometimes it will be dark but as long as we have hope there will always be a light at the end. You also meet some pretty amazing people along the way 🖤

One thing being diagnosed with cancer has taught me, is what and who is important and to cherish the little things.

Hannah Louise - @hannah_and_the_big_c

CLARE ETHERTON

@fightagainsttnbc

Water Is Your New Best Friend

Looking back what would I tell someone who has just had their biopsy results, has just heard the words "we are sorry but it is cancer" what is the advice I would share?

Firstly it would be "just breath" you will be okay, be present, take in what has just happened, take in what is being said, as much as the room will spin this information is important, everything is going to move so so fast from now, if you don't stop, calm and rationalise your mind you will struggle, after you leave the clinic go away and really research your treatments, what is your plan? start being proactive, do not research your diagnosis though, stay away from google it honestly really will not help in any way I promise you that!

This journey is about new found strengths and inner beliefs google will not give you that!

Find others on the same journey, they will be your lifelines, encouragement and inspiration, access as much support and help as possible, I was astounded by the help and support that was just thrown at me from my diagnosis, it is a sh*tty experience but I don't think you will ever truly experience kindness and strength like the journey you are about to take from the people around you going through the same.

Do not compare your treatment/journey to others there is no one that will ever be the same!

I hate to mention it but side effects from chemo are real, very real, some people breeze through it but if you do experience them know that it's your body healing and the treatments are fighting through your body killing what is trying to kill you!

Reach out to doctors and nurses as many times as you feel necessary through your treatment, ask as many questions as you need, and most importantly you will need to advocate for yourself ALOT, so get yourself prepared, just absorb as much info as possible.

You will not be the same person you once were, you will be better, stronger and more grateful, if you weren't spiritual before you might be after, don't allow your life to stop because you have had a cancer diagnosis, start planning and doing the things that you have put off!

Visualize, manifest, do what ever the hell it is that will get you through treatment!

Clare Etherton - @fightagainsttnbc

RHIANNON VICKERMAN

@breastcancerandme_bymrsv

My Story

On March 1st 2021 I went to see my GP about a lump in my breast. Two weeks later following a mammogram, ultrasound and biopsies I learnt I had breast cancer in both breasts.

I chose a bilateral mastectomy without reconstruction. I had 12 rounds of chemotherapy and 15 of radiotherapy. I'm now on hormone tablets for ten years.

I'm very grateful that I've had my treatment and that I am alive.

My survival advice

* stay positive, I read a lot and practiced the law of attraction

* do things to make you laugh and feel joyful - such as watching comedies and listening to music, anything to raise your vibe

* connect with others in similar situations, I found lots of support online

* get out in the fresh air as often as you can

* rest when you need to

* ask for help with jobs

* do the exercises they give you

* eat well, stay hydrated and prioritise sleep

* if you are having breast surgery get a litter picker, because you can't stretch your arms very far at first, it's a game changer!

#philadobook #breastcancer #bilateralmastectomy

Rhiannon Vickerman - @breastcancerandme_bymrsv

LAURA MIDDLETON-HUGHES

@baldbooblessandbeautiful

Finding The Light

After living with cancer for just under 10 years, which is almost a 3rd of my life, I have been through all the emotions you can think of. Being 25 when diagnosed with breast cancer in 2014, it turned my life upside down but nothing can prepare you for the devastation that hits when you then get the news it is incurable. This happened only a year on from finishing treatment for my primary BC. I was 28 & told the cancer had spread to my bones. In that moment I lost the career I loved, was told the dream of becoming a mother was gone & now my future was very uncertain. Life became very dark.

I often describe life like living on a rollercoaster you know you can never get off, in a very dark tunnel. You have no idea when the highs or lows will come. All you know is the track will one day run out, but you have no idea when.

But the darkness can't stay forever as over time cracks appear in the tunnel allowing moments of light in. Over time these cracks get bigger & more frequent, & in these lighter moments we find laughter, smiles & even fun again despite still living on the same rollercoaster.

Life has thrown me many challenges over the last 10 years but I try to live by my motto, 'don't worry about things you can't change'. It has helped me in many situations. I get anxious around my scans every 3 months but I try to live in the moment instead of worrying what might be in a few weeks, months time. I never thought I would still be here 7 years on which I am so grateful for, & I have done things I never thought possible

When diagnosed with secondaries instead of concentrating on the negatives of the illness, I set up a living list of all the things I wanted to do in the time I have left. This gave me things to look forward to in between treatments. I have been & done more than I ever thought possible & I know that even though life is still uncertain, I want to make the most of the time I have left.

I also set up @secondary.sisters which has been a huge support to myself & the community. It has been wonderful to give back a bit of what I have learnt over the years to those newly diagnosed.

So remember however dark life feels right now, you will find the light again.

Laura Middleton-Hughes - @baldbooblessandbeautiful

CARRIE-ANNE CALLAN

@Positivi.tittties

A Random Smattering Of (Hopefully Somewhat Useful) Thoughts

It is near on impossible to pin point exactly what caused this to happen to you. STOP trying to. Stop wondering if it's something you did. You will never know for certain. It just "is". Let it go.

This is happening, you cannot change it nor do you have control over it.

You do however have control over how you respond to it happening. So take it.

This shit is hard. No question about it.

Theres a reason people describe it as a rollercoaster. There will be many ups and downs, twists and turns. Align your expectations with this. "Happiness is equal to or greater than the events of your life, minus your expectation of how life should be" (Mo Gawdat)

You can either count, track and dwell on every negative

thing, every inconvenience, every irritation, stack them all up on top of each other one by one until the pile becomes overwhelmingly enormous and consumes you entirely OR you can accept that this shit is hard BUT it must be done and choose to seek out positives, have gratitude for the good days and the small silver linings when they occur and hey maybe even smile and feel happiness now and again . . . maybe even often, if you choose!

Every day is a push. A fight. An effort. Understand that. Some days "push" will look like simply getting from the bed to the bathroom, other days "push" will be conducting relatively normal activities.

Chemo is not meant to be easy but nor is it meant to be impossible these days. Take the meds. Ask for more if your side effects are significant. If what you are given doesn't work, ask for something different. Trial and error. There is so much help can be given, if you ask.

Drink A LOT of water. Fibre is your friend. Move your body when you can. Fresh air and nature are a tonic. Everyone's journey is different, be aware but don't compare. Eat what you can, when you can. Talking helps. Talking helps a lot. Don't stop life. Cancer is a part of who you are now but don't let it be all that you are. Keep doing the things that you love. Accept help when its offered. If you're offered a PICC line, get one. Try not to spend too much time morning the "old you", trust me, the new you is better!

Dig deep. This too shall pass.

Carrie-anne Callan - @Positivi.tittties

CHERYL THOMPSON

@ cheryl_breastcancerandme

Prior to my breast cancer diagnosis life had been for periods of time difficult. Divorce, being a single mum, self employed, trying to be the best parent I could while grieving the family I always thought I should have had, one with parents together (I no longer feel this way).

Stress, Anxiety, low moods, a lot of darkness, sometimes feeling so alone. But those things although I never knew it at the time, were all building me up with resilience because when cancer decided to pay me a visit I felt I had already survived so much. I had been picking myself up over & over for the last years. So into fight mode I went. Of course I'm only human & I have at times cried on the floor & been terrified. Let yourself do that, let that out. Then pick yourself up and pull yourself together. Appearance change can be a scary thought too, being prepared with different wigs helped me massively. Dress nice & put that bright lipstick on.

Carry on keeping up things you enjoy doing. Even on bad weeks I've got out for walks. Being out in the fresh air & just peacefully walking has been like a second medicine. Eat nourishing food but also eat what you fancy. Drink them gallons of water. Flush out the toxins. Know your own body & don't be afraid to advocate for it. I've learnt that many of the medical professionals have different ideas so make sure you let your thoughts be heard.

The person you are now isn't the same, you will have a whole better outlook on life. This person is a warrior & the strength & mindset you'll come out of this with is powerful. You'll not tolerate people moaning about insignificant things. You'll appreciate the good people around you. The ones who have quietly persistently been there. My heart is so full with love for them people. You will be surprised how different people react. Don't be disappointed by the ones you don't hear from. Let it go.

See the humour in life, laugh still. Don't let the dark thoughts take over. Focus on the things you can control. Soon this will all be over. Keep going #philaldobook #breastcancer #chemo

Cheryl Thompson - @ cheryl_breastcancerandme

MELISSA GOLDING

@melissa_golding

Audio: Break My Soul Beyonce

3 Things I Want You To Know

Hi, I'm Melissa and I was diagnosed with grade 3 ductal carcinoma in March 2020. There are many things I've learnt since, here are just three that I want to share with you.

Firstly, I googled the shit out of breast cancer as soon as I received the "no caller id" call asking me to return for a biopsy. At first at looked at everything. Then I had a word with myself and just looked at known sites, Breast Cancer Now, Macmillan, Cancer Research.

A week later, sitting in the car waiting to go in to see the breast consultant, I told my husband to prepare himself. I felt sure what I was going in to hear. I had not slept properly for a week. They had done a biopsy on the lump in my breast and my lymph nodes. I thought I was ready to some degree and had tried to mentally prepare myself.

However, hearing the words "I'm afraid to say you have breast cancer" is something I don't think you ever get over.

You cannot believe that you are "one of those people". Then the fear immediately comes and that question we all ask is "am I going to die?".

Those first few days are very hard. Telling people is so difficult and I found myself apologising to try to make them feel better. The cancer blow is huge and you can feel those ripples.

I want you to know, you absolutely are not to blame! No amount of tomatoes and other antioxidant foods would have prevented it. Don't blame yourself for having a Friday night drink or going a bit too crazy once a month. This is cancer, it's unfair, it's cruel and it doesn't discriminate.

Secondly, as great as it is to have a friend that's had breast cancer and can offer advice. Everyone is different. Your treatment plan may vary and the way you react to chemotherapy, surgery, radiotherapy can vary too. I was so scared about my first chemo session because of someone else's experience. I'm not saying it was easy but it wasn't as bad as I expected. You do you!

Thirdly, look at this as a new beginning. Once you get strong enough re-evaluate your life. Strip out anything that doesn't bring you peace or makes you happy. Consciously work on you, your goals, ambitions and hopes. Start to put yourself equal to everyone else, not last!

I am nearly 4 years on from my diagnosis and I feel my life is divided now in to "before" cancer and "after" cancer. I'm much prefer the person I am now and the life I've created. I feel I've truly lived these last few years and achieved so much more than I ever thought possible.

You've got this, chin up, straighten your invisible crown and show them who they are dealing with. 🖤

Melissa Golding - @melissa_golding

DOUG E HARPER

@doug.eharper

In 2012 I was 49 years old and the father to 4 girls, a one-year-old son and unemployed It was a frustrating time, but, cheer up things could be worse... Spoiler alert

I considered myself an average good guy, playing in bands, going to football and then my life changed in a way that I had never considered. I found out that I was different. I became one of only 300 men a year in the UK to have breast cancer three days before my 50th birthday (worse present EVAH!)

I had no idea before being diagnosed that men could get breast cancer. My partner had no idea that men could get breast cancer. My friends, my family, seemingly no one seemed to be aware that men could get breast cancer. So, I made it my life's work to raise awareness of breast cancer in men.

And what a journey it is. I have met some incredible people along the way. People that I admire, people that have made me laugh and people that make me cry, people that are an example to us all through adversity.

I have always been a glass half full type of bloke (what do you expect? I support Leyton Orient) but through this journey I have had a top up of that glass. Never say never and never say that something cannot be done (within reason or sometimes even beyond that reason).

Yes, it is bloody tough at times, but remember that there are people out there that you can talk to, people on whose shoulder you can cry on, if not friends and family then through charities and on through groups online.

When I was diagnosed, there were not a lot of resources for men but over the years thanks to a lot of work and a lot of support from charities and individuals that is changing. In the UK we now have a dedicated men's meet up group on Zoom called the Men's Virtual Meet Up, which is the first meet up for men in the country, we are now on our third year and life long friendships have been made.

Meeting with other men and women who have been through this or are going through this is emotional and there is a closeness that we all have.

I hear of many men that have been told by their GP that what they have is a cyst and to come back in six months. This of course could kill you. I know it would have killed me because I doubt, I would have gone back. So, my advice is that if you are not happy with what you are being told, then be a nuisance, demand more, after all it is your life that is being dealt. This disease does not only affect the person who has it but all of those around them so its vital that we continue to spread the message that we can all get breast cancer and to check ourselves

Much love brothers and sisters

xxxx

Doug E Harper - @doug.eharper

AFTERWORD

Embracing Tomorrow: A Collective Journey Forward

In this final chapter, we come together to reflect on the strength and resilience found within the pages of this book. We acknowledge the shared experiences, the stories of triumph, and the invaluable wisdom imparted by each contributor. Here, we emphasize the collective journey we've embarked upon—a journey shaped by hope, courage, and unity.

As we turn the final page, we don't just conclude a book; we ignite a new chapter in the lives of survivors worldwide. This isn't merely an end; it's a commencement—an invitation to carry the torch of resilience and empowerment forward.

We invite readers to take the lessons learned, the insights gained, and the connections forged beyond these pages. It's a call to action—a reminder that the stories shared within 'Someone's Survival Guide' are not just narratives; they're guiding lights, offering strength and support to those walking similar paths.

Closing with a message of hope and solidarity, we

stand together, hand in hand, in our commitment to raise awareness, promote early detection, and support those affected by breast cancer. As we bid farewell to these pages, we embrace tomorrow with renewed determination, knowing that together, we are an unstoppable force in the fight against breast cancer.

This chapter serves as both a conclusion and a call to continue the momentum generated by the collective voices within the book—a testament to the ongoing journey of empowerment, resilience, and advocacy for a brighter, cancer-free future.

#sayyesmore #gograblife #fuckthecomfortzone

@Philaldo